BELLA GEORGE

Switzerland Hiking Guide 2024

Expert Tips for Exploring Breathtaking Trails & Scenic Wonders in the Swiss Alps

First edition

This book was professionally typeset on Reedsy.
Find out more at reedsy.com

Contents

Preface

A Welcome to the Alps: Embracing the Swiss Hiking Adventure

The Alps! Breathe in the crisp mountain air, laced with the scent of pine and wildflowers. Feel the sun warm your face as you crest a rise, revealing a breathtaking panorama of emerald valleys and snow-capped peaks. The crunch of fresh snow underfoot, the rhythmic clack of hiking poles, the melody of alpine birdsong – this is the symphony of the Swiss hiking adventure.

Imagine stepping off the train in a quaint village nestled amidst verdant meadows. Cobblestone streets, charming chalets adorned with flower boxes, the sweet clink of cowbells – your senses are immediately captivated. The air feels charged with anticipation, the promise of adventure humming in the crisp breeze.

Your first steps onto the trail are invigorating. Each bend reveals a new vista, a postcard-perfect tableau of cascading waterfalls, lush forests, and glaciers glinting in the distance. The path winds through meadows carpeted with wildflowers, their vibrant hues a stark contrast to the rugged rock faces looming above.

As you climb, the air thins, invigorating your lungs and sharpening your senses. The silence is broken only by the crunch of snow underfoot and the occasional marmot's whistle. The world opens up around you, stretching impossibly vast and wild. You reach a summit, and the panorama explodes before you – a tapestry of valleys, peaks, and the azure ribbon of a distant lake. This is the moment you've been hiking for, a feeling of accomplishment and awe washing over you.

But the magic of the Swiss Alps lies not just in the breathtaking scenery. It's in the cozy mountain huts where you share stories with fellow adventurers over steaming mugs of hot cocoa. It's in the friendly smiles of locals who offer directions and share local legends. It's in the simple pleasures of a picnic lunch beside a gurgling stream, the taste of fresh bread and alpine cheese accompanied by the sweet notes of a cowbell serenade.

As the sun dips towards the horizon, painting the sky in fiery hues, you reluctantly descend. The day's journey leaves you with a sense of peace and rejuvenation, your body pleasantly tired, your spirit soaring. You carry with you not just memories, but a newfound appreciation for the simple beauty of nature, the thrill of the climb, and the camaraderie of the trail.

This is the essence of the Swiss hiking adventure. It's not just about conquering mountains; it's about embracing the journey, connecting with nature, and discovering the quiet magic that awaits along the path. So lace up your boots, pack your sense of wonder, and embark on your own alpine odyssey. The Swiss mountains are calling, and they have a story waiting to be told.

About This Guide: Your Companion for Every Step

Welcome to the ultimate guide for your Swiss hiking adventure! Whether you're a seasoned trekker or a first-time explorer, this comprehensive resource is your one-stop shop for planning an unforgettable journey through the breathtaking beauty of the Alps.

Embrace the Journey:

This guide is more than just a collection of maps and trails. It's your trusty companion, helping you navigate every step of your adventure, from choosing the perfect route to savoring the local culture. We'll provide you with:

- **In-depth trail descriptions:** Get detailed information on various hikes, including difficulty levels, distances, elevation gains, and points of interest.
- **Expert tips and advice:** Learn from seasoned hikers and local guides about gear, safety precautions, etiquette, and insider tips for maximizing your experience.
- **Cultural insights:** Immerse yourself in the rich tapestry of Swiss traditions, from charming villages and delectable cuisine to fascinating historical tidbits.
- **Inspiring stories and anecdotes:** Let the tales of fellow adventurers ignite your own wanderlust and fuel your excitement for the trail ahead.

Planning Your Perfect Hike:

With so many incredible trails to choose from, this guide will help you narrow down your options and find the perfect match for your interests and abilities. We'll cover:

- **Choosing the right region:** From the majestic peaks of the Bernese Oberland to the serene valleys of Graubünden, discover the unique character of each Alpine region.
- **Selecting the ideal trail:** Whether you seek a challenging climb, a gentle stroll through wildflowers, or a family-

friendly percorso, we'll guide you to the perfect path.

- **Finding the best time to go:** Consider the seasonal variations in weather, crowds, and trail conditions to ensure a smooth and enjoyable experience.

Enhancing Your Alpine Experience:

Beyond the trails, this guide will help you create lasting memories:

- **Unforgettable accommodations:** Discover charming mountain huts, rustic chalets, and cozy villages where you can rest your weary legs and soak in the alpine atmosphere.
- **Delicious local fare:** Savor the flavors of Switzerland, from hearty cheese dishes and fresh salads to melt-in-your-mouth pastries and steaming mugs of hot cocoa.
- **Unique cultural experiences:** Immerse yourself in local traditions, from cheese-making demonstrations and folk festivals to yodeling lessons and visits to historic landmarks.

Remember, the Swiss Alps are not just a destination; they're an adventure waiting to unfold. With this guide as your companion, you'll be equipped to embrace every step of your journey and create memories that will last a lifetime.

So lace up your boots, grab your backpack, and let's hit the trail!

I

Unveiling the Swiss Alps

The Swiss Alps are a treasure to be respected. Hike responsibly, leave no trace, and be mindful of the delicate ecosystem. By following these guidelines, you'll help preserve this magical land for generations to come.

1

Choosing Your Trails: From Gentle Rambles to Alpine Giants

The Swiss Alps offer a symphony of trails, each with its own unique melody of scenery, challenge, and charm. Whether you're a seasoned trekker seeking a heart-pounding ascent or a first-timer yearning for a leisurely stroll, finding the perfect trail is key to an unforgettable Alpine adventure. So, grab your hiking poles, loosen your laces, and let's explore the diverse terrain:

For Gentle Rambles:

- **Lake Geneva Promenade (Montreux):** Stroll along the shimmering shores of Lake Geneva, soaking in the panoramic beauty of the Lavaux vineyards and the majestic Alps. This flat, paved path is perfect for a leisurely afternoon stroll or a family outing.
- **Grindelwald First Cliff Walk:** Nestled near the idyllic Grindelwald village, this trail offers breathtaking views without the steep climb. Walk along elevated walkways bolted into the mountainside, marveling at the glaciers and

waterfalls below.

- **Lauterbrunnen Valley:** Hike through this enchanting valley, dubbed the "Valley of 72 Waterfalls." Choose from a variety of gentle paths that wind through meadows and forests, past cascading waterfalls and charming villages.

For Moderate Adventures:

- **Riffelsee - Riffelberg via Rotenboden (Zermatt):** Hike amidst the iconic Matterhorn scenery, reaching the serene Riffelsee lake reflecting the majestic peak. This moderate trail offers stunning views and a taste of the high alpine landscape.
- **Oeschinensee Lake (Kandersteg):** Take a scenic gondola ride to the emerald-green Oeschinensee lake, nestled amidst towering peaks. Hike around the lake, enjoying panoramic views and the tranquil atmosphere.
- **Männlichen Panorama Trail (Interlaken):** This easily accessible trail offers panoramic vistas of the Jungfrau region, including the Eiger and Mönch peaks. Enjoy the gentle inclines and lush meadows, perfect for a moderate afternoon hike.

For Alpine Giants:

- **Tour du Mont Blanc (TMB):** Embark on a legendary multiday trek, circumnavigating the mighty Mont Blanc massif. This challenging route traverses three countries, offering breathtaking glaciers, high passes, and unforgettable scenery.
- **Pizol Panorama Trail (Flumserberg):** Hike along a knife-

edge ridge overlooking the dramatic peaks of the Churfirsten range. This challenging trail requires good balance and sure footing, but rewards you with unparalleled views and a sense of accomplishment.

- **Klettersteig Gemmi (Kandersteg):** For experienced climbers, this via ferrata offers a thrilling ascent alongside a vertical rock face. Secured with cables and ladders, this challenging route provides an adrenaline rush and unparalleled views of the Gemmi Valley.

Remember:

- Choose trails that match your fitness level and experience. Don't underestimate the challenges of high altitudes and steep inclines.
- Research trail conditions and weather forecasts before setting off. Be prepared for changing weather and know your limits.
- Pack appropriate gear, including sturdy hiking boots, layers of clothing, and a waterproof jacket.

Bonus Tip:

- Consider hiring a local guide for challenging trails or if you're unfamiliar with the area. They can provide valuable tips, safety advice, and local knowledge.

With the right trail and preparation, your Alpine adventure awaits! Lace up your boots, choose your melody, and let the Swiss Alps guide you on an unforgettable journey.

1.1 Understanding Difficulty Levels and Terrain Types

To plan your perfect Swiss hiking adventure, understanding the difficulty levels and terrain types is crucial. Here's a breakdown:

Difficulty Levels:

The Swiss Alpine Club (SAC) defines six difficulty levels for hiking trails, ranging from easy to highly challenging:

- **T1 (Hiking):** Well-marked paths, gentle inclines, suitable for families and casual hikers.
- **T2 (Mountain Hiking):** Moderate inclines, some rougher terrain, requires basic hiking experience.
- **T3 (Demanding Mountain Hiking):** Steeper climbs, exposed sections, good fitness and surefootedness needed.
- **T4 (Alpine Hiking):** High altitudes, steep and rocky terrain, requires proper hiking boots and experience.
- **T5 (Demanding Alpine Hiking):** Very challenging routes, technical sections, scrambling might be necessary, only for experienced and well-prepared hikers.
- **T6 (Difficult Alpine Hiking):** Extremely challenging, glaciers, climbing sections, requires advanced skills and equipment, recommended with guides.

Terrain Types:

- **Trail:** Well-maintained paths with clear markings, suitable for most hikers.
- **Path:** Less defined paths, often through meadows or forests, requires some navigation skills.
- **Unmarked:** No official path, requires map and compass skills, only for experienced hikers.

- **Scramble:** Steep, rocky terrain requiring use of hands and feet, for experienced and surefooted hikers.
- **Via Ferrata:** Secured climbing route with cables and ladders, requires specialized equipment and training.
- **Glacier:** Crossing ice fields, requires crampons and proper training, often with guides.

Remember:

- Difficulty levels are subjective and can vary depending on your fitness level and experience.
- Always choose trails within your capabilities and comfort zone.
- Be aware of the terrain type and ensure you have the necessary skills and equipment.
- Check weather conditions and trail closures before setting off.

By understanding these difficulty levels and terrain types, you can choose the perfect hike for your Swiss adventure and ensure a safe and enjoyable experience.

Additional Tips:

- Use online resources like SchweizMobil or SAC maps to find detailed information about specific trails.
- Look for local guide services if you're unsure about a trail or need additional support.
- Download offline maps on your phone for navigation and safety.

Enjoy your Swiss hiking adventure!

1.2 Matching Your Skills and Preferences with the Perfect Path

Now that you understand difficulty levels and terrain types, let's match your skills and preferences with the perfect Alpine path! Here's how:

First, Tell Me About Yourself:

1. **Experience:** Are you a seasoned trekker or a first-time explorer? How comfortable are you navigating different terrains and inclines?
2. **Fitness Level:** Do you enjoy daily workouts, or are you more comfortable with leisurely walks? Be honest about your stamina and potential fatigue.
3. **Adventure Seeking:** Do you crave adrenaline-pumping climbs or prefer scenic strolls with breathtaking views? How much challenge are you looking for?
4. **Time and Pace:** Do you have a full day for a demanding trek or prefer shorter, half-day explorations? Choose a path that matches your timeframe.
5. **Scenic Preferences:** Do you dream of glacier crossings or lush meadows? Are waterfalls or panoramic vistas your calling? Prioritize your desired landscape.

Now, Let's Find Your Path:

With your answers in mind, here are some potential matches:

For Moderate Adventure Seekers:

- **Grindelwald First Cliff Walk:** Enjoy breathtaking views of glaciers and waterfalls without a steep climb. (T2, path)
- **Riffelsee - Riffelberg via Rotenboden (Zermatt):** Hike

amidst iconic Matterhorn scenery towards a serene lake reflecting the majestic peak. (T2, trail)

· **Oeschinensee Lake (Kandersteg):** Take a gondola ride to a stunning emerald lake and hike around its scenic shores. (T2, trail)

For Experienced Thrill Seekers:

· **Tour du Mont Blanc (TMB):** Embark on a multi-day trek for seasoned adventurers, with glaciers, high passes, and stunning scenery across three countries. (T3-T4, various terrain)
· **Pizol Panorama Trail (Flumserberg):** Challenge yourself on a knife-edge ridge with unparalleled views, requiring good balance and surefootedness. (T3, exposed ridge)
· **Klettersteig Gemmi (Kandersteg):** For skilled climbers, this via ferrata offers a thrilling ascent alongside a vertical rock face. (T4-T5, via ferrata)

For Nature Lovers Seeking Tranquility:

· **Lake Geneva Promenade (Montreux):** Stroll along the shimmering lake, soaking in the beauty of vineyards and majestic Alps. (T1, paved path)
· **Lauterbrunnen Valley:** Hike through the "Valley of 72 Waterfalls," choosing from gentle paths that wind through meadows and charming villages. (T1-T2, various trails)
· **Männlichen Panorama Trail (Interlaken):** Enjoy panoramic vistas of the Jungfrau region on this easily accessible trail, with gentle inclines and lush meadows. (T2, trail)

Remember:

- These are just suggestions; always choose a trail that matches your specific skills and preferences.
- Don't hesitate to adjust your plans based on your fitness level and weather conditions.
- Enjoy the journey as much as the destination! Soak in the Alpine magic and embrace the unexpected encounters.

With careful planning and self-awareness, you're guaranteed to find the perfect Swiss hiking path that matches your heart's desire. Happy trails!

1.3 Planning Family-Friendly and Accessible Excursions

The Swiss Alps aren't just for seasoned trekkers; families and accessibility-minded individuals can create their own magical Alpine adventures too! Here are some tips for planning family-friendly and accessible excursions:

Family Fun:

- **Gondola and Train Adventures:** Opt for scenic rides up mountain peaks like First or Mt. Rigi instead of challenging hikes. Enjoy breathtaking views, playgrounds, and family-friendly restaurants at the summit.
- **Themenwege:** Follow themed trails with interactive elements, like learning about local flora and fauna or solving riddles along the way. Check out the "Märchenweg" near Engelberg or the "Gletscherlehrpfad" near Grindelwald.
- **Water Activities:** Take a boat trip on a serene lake like

Oeschinen or Brienz, swim in a refreshing mountain lake, or visit a waterfall like Staubbachfall.

- **Playground Paradise:** Many villages and mountaintop restaurants boast fantastic playgrounds where kids can burn off energy while parents relax.
- **Cultural Activities:** Visit cheese and chocolate factories, learn about traditional crafts, or take a family-friendly hike with a local guide who can share stories and legends.

Accessibility Matters:

- **Wheelchair-Accessible Trails:** Choose designated accessible trails like the Männlichen Panorama Trail near Grindelwald or the Seeweg am Lungernsee. Many towns offer wheelchair-friendly routes and facilities.
- **Cable Cars and Gondolas:** Many gondolas and cable cars are wheelchair-accessible, providing breathtaking views without the physical exertion. Check accessibility information beforehand.
- **Accessible Accommodations:** Choose hotels and restaurants with designated accessible rooms and facilities. Look for the "Handicap Service" symbol.
- **Planning and Preparation:** Research routes and transportation options for accessibility. Inform restaurants and activities in advance if any specific needs require attention.
- **Adaptive Equipment:** Consider utilizing hiking poles, backpacks with ergonomic support, or even specialized all-terrain wheelchairs for comfortable exploration.

Remember:

- Pace yourselves and prioritize short, enjoyable hikes to keep everyone engaged.
- Pack snacks, water, and sun protection for the whole family.
- Wear comfortable clothes and shoes suitable for uneven terrain.
- Download offline maps and emergency contact information on your phone.
- Most importantly, relax, have fun, and create lasting memories together!

The Swiss Alps offer something for everyone, and with proper planning and consideration, families and accessibility-minded individuals can embark on their own unique and unforgettable Alpine adventures. So, lace up your walking shoes, pack your sense of wonder, and let the mountains embrace you all!

2

Gearing Up for Success: Essential Equipment and Clothing

Conquering the Swiss Alps requires more than just enthusiasm; proper equipment and clothing are crucial for a safe and comfortable journey. So, whether you're a seasoned trekker or a first-timer embarking on a gentle stroll, pack these essentials for your Alpine odyssey:

Essential Gear:

- **Backpack:** Choose a comfortable, well-fitting backpack with enough capacity for your supplies (20-28 liters for day hikes, 50+ liters for multi-day treks). Rain cover and hip belt are essential features.
- **Hiking boots:** Invest in sturdy, waterproof boots with good ankle support and traction. Consider the terrain and weather conditions when choosing your boots.
- **Hiking poles:** These provide stability and support, especially on steep inclines and difficult terrain. Optional, but

highly recommended for most hikes.

- **Map and compass:** Download offline maps on your phone for navigation, but always carry a physical map and compass as backup. Learn how to use them before setting off.
- **First-aid kit:** Be prepared for minor injuries with a well-stocked kit containing bandages, antiseptic wipes, pain relievers, and other essentials.
- **Headlamp:** Even day hikes might encounter nightfall, so pack a reliable headlamp for emergencies.
- **Sun protection:** Sunglasses, sunscreen with high SPF, and a hat are vital for protecting yourself from the sun's harsh rays at high altitudes.
- **Water bottle and hydration bladder:** Stay hydrated throughout the day with at least 2 liters of water. Consider a hydration bladder for easy access.
- **Snacks and food:** Pack energy-rich snacks like nuts, fruits, and granola bars, and nutritious meals for longer hikes.
- **Knife and multi-tool:** These can be handy for various tasks like cutting fruit or fixing minor gear issues.
- **Emergency whistle:** Attract attention in case of emergencies.

Clothing Essentials:

- **Base layer:** Pack moisture-wicking base layers made from merino wool or synthetic materials to keep you comfortable and dry.
- **Mid-layer:** Fleeces or lightweight sweaters provide warmth and insulation. Choose layers you can easily add or remove depending on the weather.
- **Hiking pants:** Breathable and durable pants suitable for the

terrain are crucial. Convertible pants offer both long and short options.

- **Rain jacket and pants:** A waterproof and breathable rain jacket and pants are essential for unpredictable mountain weather.
- **Windbreaker:** A lightweight windbreaker provides additional protection against wind and light rain.
- **Hat and gloves:** Pack a warm hat and gloves for colder temperatures and higher altitudes.
- **Hiking socks:** Moisture-wicking socks prevent blisters and ensure comfort on the trail.
- **Sun shirt:** Long-sleeved sun shirts with UPF protection provide sun protection and keep you cool.

Additional Tips:

- Consider the specific weather conditions and activities planned when choosing your gear and clothing.
- Layer your clothing for adjustability based on changing temperatures.
- Pack lightweight and quick-drying materials for efficient movement and comfort.
- Don't forget sunglasses, sunscreen, and lip balm for essential sun protection.
- Break in your hiking boots before your trip to avoid blisters.
- Check local regulations regarding certain equipment requirements for specific trails.

Remember: Proper gear and clothing can make a significant difference in your Alpine experience. By packing wisely and preparing for various weather conditions, you'll ensure a safe, comfortable, and memorable journey through the breathtaking Swiss Alps. So, pack your essentials, lace up your boots, and embrace the mountain magic!

2.1 Selecting Sturdy Footwear and Layering for Varied Conditions

The beauty of the Swiss Alps lies in their diverse landscapes and ever-changing weather. To conquer peaks and valleys in comfort and confidence, choosing the right footwear and layering strategy is key. Here's how to prepare for the varied conditions:

Footwear:

- **Terrain:** Consider the terrain you'll be tackling. Choose sturdy hiking boots with good ankle support and Vibram soles for uneven paths and rocky hikes. Opt for lightweight trail runners with good traction for gentler trails.
- **Weather:** Waterproof boots are essential for unpredictable mountain rain or snow. Consider insulated boots for high altitudes or winter hikes.
- **Fit:** Boots should fit snugly but not uncomfortably. Try them on with hiking socks to ensure optimal fit and prevent blisters.
- **Break-in:** Don't wait until your trip to break in your boots! Wear them around town or on short hikes to avoid discomfort on the trail.

Layering:

- **Base Layer:** Moisture-wicking merino wool or synthetic

base layers are critical for regulating temperature and staying dry. Choose long sleeves and pants for additional warmth.

- **Mid-Layer:** Fleeces or light sweaters provide insulation and can be easily layered or removed depending on the weather. Consider zip-ups for better ventilation.
- **Insulating Layer:** Down jackets or synthetic puffy jackets offer warmth for colder temperatures or higher altitudes. Pack a packable option for easy storage.
- **Shell Layer:** A waterproof and breathable rain jacket and pants are crucial for protection against rain, snow, and wind. Choose lightweight, packable options with good ventilation.
- **Sun Protection:** A long-sleeved sun shirt with UPF protection is essential to shield you from the harsh sun, especially at high altitudes. Wear a wide-brimmed hat and sunglasses for added protection.

Adapting to Changing Conditions:

- **The Onion Principle:** Layer your clothing so you can easily add or remove items as the temperature or activity level changes.
- **Pack Extras:** Bring a dry base layer and socks in case of unexpected rain or snow.
- **Stay Dry:** Wet clothes lose their insulating properties, so prioritize staying dry by changing wet layers promptly.
- **Listen to Your Body:** Adapt your clothing choices based on how you feel. Don't hesitate to add or remove layers to maintain comfort.

Remember: Choosing the right footwear and layering strategy is key to a comfortable and enjoyable Swiss Alpine adventure. By considering the terrain, weather, and your personal needs, you can navigate the diverse conditions with confidence and embrace the mountain magic, no matter what the weather throws your way.

Happy trails!

2.2 Navigation Tools and Maps: Staying on Track in the Mountains

Getting lost in the breathtaking beauty of the Swiss Alps might sound romantic, but in reality, staying on track is crucial for safety and a satisfying adventure. Here's how to navigate like a pro:

Essential Tools:

- **Map and Compass:** This classic combo remains indispensable, even with the rise of digital options. Choose a detailed paper map of the region and learn basic compass navigation before setting off.
- **Phone with Offline Maps:** Download offline maps and hiking apps like SchweizMobil or SwissMaps on your phone for GPS tracking and route guidance. Ensure your phone has enough battery and consider a portable charger.
- **Altimeter and Barometer:** These tools can provide valuable information about altitude and weather changes, especially helpful in high-altitude terrain.
- **GPS Device:** Dedicated GPS devices offer reliable navigation even in low signal areas. Consider renting one if you're unfamiliar with the area or tackling challenging routes.

Map Reading Skills:

- **Map Scale:** Understand the map scale to interpret distances and plan your route accurately.
- **Symbols and Legend:** Familiarize yourself with the symbols used on the map for trails, landmarks, and potential hazards.
- **Contour Lines:** Learn to read contour lines to understand the terrain, elevation changes, and potential risks like steep slopes or ravines.

Trail Blazing Tips:

- **Plan Your Route:** Research the trail beforehand, noting key points like junctions, landmarks, and estimated times. Mark your route on the map and share it with someone back home for safety precautions.
- **Stay on Marked Trails:** Always prioritize official hiking trails unless you have the necessary experience and skills for off-trail navigation.
- **Use Waypoints:** Mark crucial points on your map or GPS device, like rest stops, water sources, or tricky junctions, to aid navigation.
- **Track Your Progress:** Regularly check your map and GPS to monitor your location and ensure you're on the right track. Don't hesitate to backtrack if you're unsure.
- **Be Aware of Your Surroundings:** Pay attention to trail markers, natural landmarks, and changes in terrain. Don't rely solely on your map or device.

Emergency Preparedness:

- **Download emergency contact information:** Save local emergency numbers (REGA - Swiss Air Rescue) on your phone, even if offline.
- **Carry a whistle and first-aid kit:** Be prepared for minor injuries and attract attention in case of emergencies.
- **Dress for changeable weather:** Pack layers and rain gear, even for short hikes, as mountain weather can shift quickly.
- **Inform Someone of Your Plans:** Share your planned route and estimated return time with someone back home for peace of mind and potential rescue assistance.

Remember: Navigation isn't just about finding your way; it's about safety and a responsible approach to exploring the mountains. By mastering basic skills, utilizing reliable tools, and staying alert, you can navigate the Swiss Alps with confidence and unlock the true magic of their diverse landscapes. Happy exploring!

2.3 First-Aid Kit and Essentials for Safety and Peace of Mind

Conquering the Swiss Alps is an exhilarating adventure, but it's crucial to be prepared for unexpected bumps and scrapes along the way. A well-stocked first-aid kit provides peace of mind and allows you to handle minor injuries efficiently, ensuring your Alpine journey remains worry-free. Here's what to pack for optimal preparedness:

Essential Supplies:

- **Wound care:** Sterile bandages in various sizes, gauze pads, adhesive tape, butterfly closures, antiseptic wipes, tweezers, safety pins.

- **Pain relief:** Pain relievers like Ibuprofen or Paracetamol, aspirin (consult doctor if on blood thinners).
- **Blister care:** Moleskin, blister pads, blister balm.
- **Antihistamines:** For allergic reactions to insect bites or stings.
- **Eye care:** Eye drops for irritation or debris removal.
- **Gastrointestinal relief:** Medication for upset stomach or diarrhea (consult doctor for specific recommendations).
- **Sunscreen and insect repellent:** Protect yourself from sunburn and insect bites.
- **Personal medications:** Pack any prescription medications you require.

Additional Considerations:

- **Size and Weight:** Choose a compact and lightweight kit that's easy to carry in your backpack.
- **Organization:** Pack items logically and label compartments for easy access.
- **Instructions:** Include basic instructions for common injuries and medication use.
- **Personalize it:** Tailor the kit to your specific needs and potential hiking hazards.
- **Expiry Dates:** Regularly check and restock expired items.

Beyond the Kit:

- **Knowledge:** Learn basic first-aid skills like wound cleaning, CPR, and splinting before your trip.
- **Emergency Preparedness:** Know emergency contact num-

bers (REGA - Swiss Air Rescue) and download offline maps for easier communication and assistance.

- **Risk Assessment:** Identify potential hazards on your chosen trail and pack additional supplies accordingly, like extra bandages for rocky terrain or electrolyte tablets for high-altitude hikes.
- **Prevention is Key:** Wear appropriate footwear, avoid sun exposure during peak hours, and stay hydrated to minimize the risk of injuries and illnesses.

Remember: A first-aid kit is an essential part of your Alpine gear, but it's not a substitute for good judgment and caution. By combining preparedness with responsible hiking practices, you can transform minor setbacks into minor inconveniences and ensure your Swiss adventure remains one to cherish.

Happy and safe trails!

3

Logistics and Accommodation: Where to Stay and How to Get Around

Unveiling the majestic Swiss Alps is just the beginning of your adventure. Where to stay and how to get around are crucial parts of the puzzle, shaping the rhythm and character of your Alpine odyssey. Here's how to navigate the logistics and unlock a seamlessly connected journey:

Accommodation:

- **Charming Villages:** Nestled amidst valleys and meadows, traditional Alpine villages offer cozy chalets, guesthouses, and family-run hotels. Immerse yourself in local charm, savor hearty meals, and enjoy breathtaking views from your doorstep.
- **Mountain Resorts:** For panoramic vistas and convenient access to ski slopes or hiking trails, choose mountain resorts. These often offer a range of amenities, from spa treatments to swimming pools, catering to various budgets and preferences.
- **Unique Options:** Consider glamping in luxurious tents with

spectacular views, staying in historic mountain huts for an authentic experience, or booking a charming room in a converted monastery.

- **Planning Tips:** Choose your location based on your planned activities and desired atmosphere. Book well in advance, especially during peak seasons. Consider eco-friendly options and local guesthouses for a more authentic experience.

Getting Around:

- **Trains and Buses:** Switzerland boasts an extensive and efficient public transportation system. Trains whisk you through breathtaking landscapes, while buses navigate smaller villages and mountainside roads. Purchase travel passes for multi-day journeys and enjoy hassle-free exploration.
- **Cable Cars and Gondolas:** Soar above valleys and reach majestic peaks in minutes. Scenic cable car rides offer stunning views and convenient access to hiking trails and mountain restaurants.
- **Walking and Hiking:** Lace up your boots and embrace the rhythm of your own steps. Many picturesque villages and landscapes are best explored on foot, allowing you to soak in the natural beauty and local charm at your own pace.
- **Biking:** For the adventurous souls, renting a bike unlocks freedom and scenic exploration. Discover hidden valleys, conquer mountain passes, or coast down gently sloping trails, enjoying the wind in your hair and the panorama unfolding before you.

Planning Your Journey:

- **Research travel options:** Check train and bus schedules, gondola accessibility, and local hiking routes beforehand.
- **Consider travel passes:** Multi-day passes offer convenience and cost savings for extensive travel.
- **Combine different modes:** Create a dynamic itinerary mixing trains, buses, cable cars, and hikes for a diverse and exciting experience.
- **Factor in travel time:** Account for potential delays or connections when planning your daily agenda.
- **Embrace spontaneity:** Leave room for serendipitous discoveries and detours – you might stumble upon a hidden gem along the way!

Remember: Logistics are like the threads weaving your Alpine adventure together. By choosing the right accommodation and transportation options, you can create a seamless and enriching journey, filled with unforgettable experiences and memories that will last a lifetime. So, explore, connect, and let the rhythm of the mountains guide you!

Happy travels!

3.1 Choosing Lodging Options: Mountain Huts, Cozy Villages, or Chic Retreats

The Alpine abode! Choosing your Swiss accommodation is not just about shelter, it's about setting the stage for your adventure. Each option offers a unique ambience and experience, so dive into these enticing possibilities:

Mountain Huts:

- **For the Adventurers:** Embrace rustic charm and a sense of camaraderie at these high-altitude havens. Share bunk beds with fellow trekkers, savor hearty meals by the crackling fireplace, and wake up to sunrises that paint the peaks in gold.

- **Location, Location, Location:** Nestled near glaciers, nestled amidst stunning landscapes, or perched on secluded ridges, mountain huts provide unparalleled access to hiking trails and breathtaking views.
- **Simple yet Authentic:** Expect basic amenities and shared facilities, but be rewarded with an immersion into local culture and unforgettable stories shared under the starry sky.
- **Things to Consider:** Booking well in advance is crucial, especially during peak season. Be prepared for limited personal space and potential snoring neighbors. Pack essentials like a sleeping bag liner and headlamps.

Cozy Villages:

- **Charming Ambiance:** Wander through cobbled streets lined with pastel-colored houses, adorned with blooming window boxes. Savor local delicacies at quaint cafes, soak in the relaxed atmosphere, and feel the warmth of community spirit.
- **Base Camp for Exploration:** Villages offer convenient access to various activities, from gentle valley hikes to scenic cable car rides. Explore nearby shops and museums, discover hidden waterfalls, and lose yourself in the rhythm of mountain life.
- **Comfort and Choice:** Choose from family-run guesthouses offering warm hospitality to comfortable hotels with mod-

ern amenities. Enjoy cozy evenings by the fireplace and wake up to the scent of freshly baked bread.

- **Things to Consider:** Villages might be less secluded than mountain huts. Noise levels can vary depending on location and season. Factor in potential travel time if your planned activities are further afield.

Chic Retreats:

- **Indulgence in the Alps:** Pamper yourself in luxurious spas, savor gourmet meals in Michelin-starred restaurants, and bask in the breathtaking scenery from infinity pools. These chic retreats offer a sophisticated escape without compromising on Alpine charm.
- **Modern Design Meets Nature:** Expect sleek architecture seamlessly integrated with stunning landscapes. Enjoy private balconies with panoramic views, designer furnishings, and state-of-the-art amenities.
- **Tailored Experiences:** Concierge services curate bespoke adventures, from private guided hikes to helicopter tours. Unwind in an atmosphere of elegance and personalized attention.
- **Things to Consider:** Chic retreats often come with a higher price tag. Check if activities and meals are included or require additional costs. Book well in advance, especially during peak season.

Remember: Choose your Alpine abode based on your desired experience, budget, and travel style. Whether you crave rustic charm, village warmth, or sophisticated indulgence, find the perfect setting to unwind, recharge, and create lasting Alpine memories. So, breathe in the crisp mountain air, and let your Swiss adventure begin!

Happy dreaming!

3.2 Public Transportation and Trailhead Access: Connecting the Dots

The conundrum of connecting the dots – from bustling train stations to idyllic trailheads nestled deep in the Swiss embrace. Fear not, for public transportation in Switzerland is a marvel, weaving a web of connections to unlock the secrets of the Alps. Here's your guide to navigating this system and seamlessly reaching your hiking haven:

Planning Your Journey:

- **Maps and Apps:** Befriend SchweizMobil (https://www.sc hweizmobil.ch/) and Swiss Railways (https://www.sbb.ch/) as your trusted allies. These websites and apps offer detailed information about train and bus schedules, cable car connections, and trailhead accessibility.
- **Start and End Points:** Clearly define your starting point (train station, village) and desired trailhead. Research available public transportation options and potential connections.
- **Time is of the Essence:** Factor in travel time between stations, potential bus or cable car connections, and hiking time to the trailhead. Consider early departures to avoid crowds and ensure enough daylight for your hike.

Navigating the Network:

- **Trains and Buses:** Switzerland boasts an extensive and punctual railway network, often reaching charming villages tucked away in valleys. Buses connect smaller towns and remote areas, providing access to hidden gems and secluded trailheads.
- **Cable Cars and Gondolas:** These magical contraptions whisk you effortlessly up mountain sides, revealing breathtaking panoramas and depositing you closer to your hiking paradise. Research operating hours and ticket options beforehand.
- **Trailhead Access:** Not all trailheads are directly accessible by public transportation. Be prepared for short walks or hikes from bus stops or cable car stations. Download offline maps on your phone for navigation and safety.

Pro Tips:

- **Travel Passes:** Consider purchasing regional or national travel passes for multi-day journeys, offering cost savings and convenience.
- **Timetables and Updates:** Check real-time schedules and potential disruptions before setting off. Download offline timetables for peace of mind on remote routes.
- **Combine and Conquer:** Don't hesitate to mix and match transportation options. Taking a scenic train ride followed by a cable car ascent can transform your journey into an adventure in itself.
- **Ask the Locals:** Tourist offices and locals are wealths of knowledge. Don't hesitate to inquire about specific routes, connections, or hidden gems waiting to be discovered.

Remember: Public transportation in Switzerland is your gateway to countless Alpine adventures. By planning your journey effectively, utilizing available resources, and embracing the flexibility of the network, you can seamlessly connect the dots and unlock the breathtaking trails and enchanting landscapes that await. So, lace up your boots, grab your map, and let the mountains embrace you!

Happy trails!

3.3 Sustainable Travel Tips: Respecting the Local Environment and Culture

Conquering the Swiss Alps shouldn't just be about personal conquest; it's about responsible exploration and leaving a positive footprint on the land and its people. Here are some sustainable travel tips to minimize your impact and maximize your connection with this magical region:

Minimize Your Footprint:

- **Reduce waste:** Pack reusable water bottles, snacks in reusable containers, and avoid single-use plastics. Minimize packaging waste when buying groceries or souvenirs.
- **Conserve water:** Take shorter showers, use water-efficient appliances in your accommodation, and avoid unnecessary water consumption.
- **Travel responsibly:** Choose public transportation or electric vehicles whenever possible. Opt for local and organic food in restaurants to support sustainable agriculture.
- **Respect wildlife:** Observe animals from a safe distance, avoid disturbing their habitats, and never litter or leave food

behind.

Embrace Responsible Hospitality:

- **Support local businesses:** Choose locally owned accommodations, restaurants, and shops to contribute to the community's economy and preserve cultural heritage.
- **Learn a few phrases:** Basic greetings and essential terms in German, French, or Italian show respect and appreciation for the local culture.
- **Mind your manners:** Be mindful of local customs and traditions. Respect public spaces, maintain noise levels, and dress appropriately when visiting religious sites.
- **Leave no trace:** Always dispose of waste properly, minimize noise disruptions, and leave hiking trails and natural areas untouched.

Connecting with the Community:

- **Engage with locals:** Strike up conversations with shopkeepers, restaurant staff, or fellow travelers. Share stories, learn about local traditions, and gain deeper insights into the Alpine way of life.
- **Support responsible tourism initiatives:** Look for hotels or activities with sustainability certifications or programs that support local communities and environmental conservation.
- **Volunteer your time:** Consider volunteering for trail maintenance or environmental projects during your trip. It's a rewarding way to give back and contribute to the well-being of the region.

· **Spread the word:** Share your responsible travel experiences and encourage others to embrace sustainable practices when exploring the Swiss Alps.

Remember: Sustainable travel is about respecting the environment, supporting local communities, and ensuring future generations can enjoy the same Alpine magic we experience today. By incorporating these tips into your journey, you can create a positive impact and leave a lasting legacy of responsible exploration in the heart of the mountains.

So, pack your sense of adventure, your respect for nature, and your desire to connect with the local spirit. The Swiss Alps await, ready to unfold their secrets to those who tread with a responsible heart.

Happy and sustainable travels!

II

Planning Your Swiss Odyssey:

The Swiss Alps whisper your name, beckoning you with promises of breathtaking panoramas, invigorating climbs, and cozy evenings by crackling fires. But before you lace up your boots and embark on your odyssey, a little planning goes a long way in ensuring a safe, enjoyable, and unforgettable adventure.

4

Peaks and Panoramas: Iconic Hikes for Unforgettable Views

The call of the Alps! Your boots are itching, your lungs crave crisp mountain air, and your soul yearns for breathtaking panoramas. Let's dive into the realm of iconic Swiss hikes, where every step rewards you with unforgettable vistas and memories etched in stone:

For the Glacier Gazers:

- **Aletsch Panoramaweg:** Embark on a majestic journey alongside the mighty Aletsch Glacier, the largest in Europe. This moderate 23km trail winds through idyllic alpine meadows, past shimmering glacial lakes, and culminates in the breathtaking Jungfrau panorama.

For the Ridge Runners:

- **First-Bachalpsee:** Conquering the First Ridge might sound daunting, but the panoramic views from this moderate 6km trail are pure magic. Traverse grassy ridges, spot marmots frolicking in the sun, and gaze upon glistening turquoise lakes nestled amidst emerald valleys.

For the Waterfall Wanderers:

- **Lauterbrunnen-Trümmelbachfälle:** This moderate 6km trail is a symphony of water and rock. Hike through lush forests, witness the thunderous Staubbachfall cascading down a cliff face, and delve into the heart of the Trümmelbachfälle, a series of subterranean waterfalls hidden within the mountain.

For the History Buffs:

- **Grand St. Bernard Pass:** Lace up your boots for a moderate 22km historical trek. Follow in the footsteps of Roman legions, admire the iconic St. Bernard dogs, and soak in the panoramic views of Mont Blanc and the Italian Val d'Aosta.

For the Family Fun Seekers:

- **Rigi Kaltbad-Scheidegg:** This easy 4km trail is perfect for families. Take the cogwheel train up Rigi, enjoy panoramic vistas of Lake Lucerne and the surrounding peaks, and let the kids loose on the scenic Spielbodenalp playground.

For the Thrill Seekers:

- **Via Ferrata Engelstock:** This challenging 3km via ferrata offers adrenaline-pumping thrills for experienced climbers. Secured by cables and ladders, ascend sheer rock faces, traverse exposed ridges, and conquer your fear of heights with breathtaking rewards.

Remember: Choose a hike that matches your fitness level and experience. Research weather conditions and trail information beforehand. Pack essentials like water, sunscreen, and snacks. Leave no trace and respect the fragile alpine environment.
   Beyond the trails:

- Explore charming mountain villages.
- Sample local cheeses and chocolates.
- Soak in a thermal bath with panoramic views.
- Take a scenic cable car ride.
- Immerse yourself in the vibrant culture.

The Swiss Alps offer a symphony of experiences beyond the trails. Let the mountains guide you, embrace the adventure, and create memories that will forever echo in your soul.
   Happy hiking!

4.1 The Matterhorn: Conquering the Crown Jewel of the Alps

The Matterhorn, with its majestic pyramid peak piercing the sky, reigns supreme as the crown jewel of the Alps. Ascending this iconic mountain is a dream for many, but it's not a trek to take lightly. Here's everything you need to know to experience the Matterhorn, from choosing the right route to ensuring a safe and unforgettable adventure:
   Know Your Options:

- **Hiking the Hörnli Ridge:** This classic route, with its steep ascents, exposed sections, and glacial crossings, is for experienced mountaineers only. Requires technical skills, glacier equipment, and proper guidance.
- **Panorama Hiking Around the Matterhorn:** Several trails, like the Matterhorn Glacier Trail and the Five Lake Walk, offer stunning views of the mountain without the technical challenges. Perfect for hikers of all levels seeking breath-taking panoramas.
- **Taking the Cable Cars:** Embrace the breathtaking scenery from the comfort of cable cars reaching Schwarzsee Paradise and Trockener Steg. Enjoy panoramic views, restaurants, and glacier hikes without strenuous climbs.

Planning and Preparation:

- **Start Early:** Climbing season is short (July–September), so book accommodation and guides well in advance. Plan your ascent to reach the summit before noon due to potential afternoon storms.
- **Hire a Guide:** Unless you're a seasoned mountaineer, always hire a certified mountain guide for the Hörnli Ridge. They'll assess your skills, provide essential safety knowledge, and navigate the challenging terrain.
- **Train and Equip Yourself:** Build physical fitness and endurance for the demanding climb. Practice using crampons and ice axes. Invest in proper mountaineering gear and clothing suitable for extreme conditions.
- **Weather Watch:** Check weather forecasts diligently and be prepared for sudden changes. Turn back if conditions become unsafe.

Respect the Mountain:

- **The Matterhorn is not just a challenge, it's a mighty force of nature.** Respect its power and prioritize safety over reaching the summit at all costs.
- **Leave no trace:** Pack out all your waste and minimize your impact on the fragile alpine environment.
- **Share the trails:** Be courteous to other hikers and climbers, especially on narrow sections.

Beyond the Climb:

- **Hike the surrounding trails:** Explore the Five Lake Walk, the Matterhorn Glacier Trail, or the Theodul Pass for stunning views and a range of difficulty levels.
- **Visit Zermatt:** Immerse yourself in the charming village nestled at the foot of the Matterhorn. Explore museums, shops, and indulge in delicious local cuisine.
- **Take a scenic Gondola ride:** Ascend to viewpoints like Schwarzsee Paradise or Trockener Steg for awe-inspiring panoramas without the physical exertion.

Remember: Conquering the Matterhorn is a privilege, not a right. Prepare meticulously, respect the mountain, and prioritize safety above all else. Whether you reach the summit or not, the Matterhorn will leave an indelible mark on your soul, a testament to your courage and connection with the awe-inspiring power of nature.

Happy and safe adventures in the shadow of the Matterhorn!

4.2 Jungfraujoch: A Journey to the Top of Europe

The Jungfraujoch, nestled amidst the mighty peaks of the Bernese Alps, holds the alluring title of "Top of Europe," beckoning travelers with its promise of breathtaking views and alpine enchantment. But preparing for this extraordinary journey requires more than just packing your hiking boots. Here's your guide to navigating the Jungfraujoch experience:

Reaching the Summit:

- **Scenic Train Ride:** The Jungfrau railway, a marvel of engineering, whisks you through enchanting landscapes to Europe's highest railway station. Witness glaciers, waterfalls, and charming villages along the way.
- **Time Your Trip:** Choose weekdays if possible, as weekends tend to be more crowded. Consider early morning departures for a less hectic experience.
- **Tickets and Prices:** Book your tickets online in advance, especially during peak season. Be aware of the different ticket options and choose the one that suits your needs and budget.

Experiencing the Jungfraujoch:

- **Breathtaking Panoramas:** Step onto the Sphinx Observation Terrace and be awestruck by the 360-degree views of the Eiger, Mönch, Jungfrau, and other majestic peaks.
- **Ice Palace:** Explore the Ice Palace, a world of sculpted ice and light, carved into the heart of the glacier. This unique experience lets you touch the very soul of the mountain.
- **Alpine Sensation:** Embark on a virtual journey through the

history and geology of the Jungfrau region in the Alpine Sensation multimedia exhibition.

- **Dining with a View:** Indulge in a delicious meal at one of the restaurants, savoring traditional Swiss cuisine while soaking in the panoramic vistas.

Beyond the Summit:

- **Kleine Scheidegg:** Explore this charming mountain village, offering breathtaking views and access to various hiking trails.
- **Grindelwald:** Discover a picturesque village full of charm and adventure, with activities like paragliding, canyoning, and glacier hiking.
- **Lauterbrunnen Valley:** Immerse yourself in the enchanting Lauterbrunnen Valley, known for its cascading waterfalls and lush meadows.

Planning Tips:

- **Dress for the weather:** Prepare for cold temperatures and high altitude conditions, even in summer. Bring layers, sunglasses, sunscreen, and a hat.
- **Consider your fitness level:** While the main experience is accessible by train, several hiking trails offer various difficulty levels around the Jungfraujoch.
- **Time Management:** Allocate enough time for the train journey, exploring the Jungfraujoch, and any additional activities you plan.

Remember: The Jungfraujoch is a unique and unforgettable experience. By planning your trip carefully, respecting the fragile alpine environment, and embracing the wonder of the scenery, you'll create memories that will last a lifetime.

So, take a deep breath of crisp mountain air, prepare for the breathtaking views, and get ready to reach the Top of Europe! Happy adventures!

4.3 Glacier 3000: A Surreal World of Snow, Ice, and Alpine Delights

Nestled amidst the Vaud Alps, Glacier 3000 isn't just a stunning alpine destination; it's a portal to a surreal world where snow, ice, and exhilarating activities collide. Whether you're a thrill-seeker or a nature enthusiast, Glacier 3000 offers something for everyone, inviting you to create memories that will forever shimmer like Alpine glaciers.

A Playground for All:

- **Peak Walk by Tissot:** For a taste of adrenaline, step onto the world's highest suspension bridge, connecting two peaks and offering dizzying views of the Diablerets massif and beyond.
- **Alpine Coaster:** Let your inner child loose on the exhilarating Funpark Coaster, weaving through lush meadows and breathtaking landscapes at hair-raising speeds.
- **Glacier Walk:** Embark on a guided journey onto the pristine surface of the Glacier 3000, feeling the raw power of nature beneath your feet and witnessing mesmerizing ice formations.
- **Hiking and Adventure:** Explore a network of hiking trails catering to all levels, from gentle strolls around Lake Louché

to challenging climbs offering panoramic vistas.

- **Chill and Dine:** Savor delicious local cuisine at one of the mountain restaurants, reveling in the spectacular scenery while warming up with a steaming hot chocolate.

Beyond the Activities:

- **Sunsets of Mythical Beauty:** Witness the sun setting over the Diablerets, painting the sky in a symphony of fiery hues that will leave you breathless.
- **Stargazing at Dizzying Heights:** Escape the light pollution and immerse yourself in the mesmerizing spectacle of the Milky Way from Europe's highest astronomical observatory.
- **Cultural Delights:** Explore the charming village of Les Diablerets, known for its traditional architecture and welcoming atmosphere. Sample local cheeses and indulge in authentic Swiss cuisine.

Planning Your Escape:

- **Accessibility:** Easily accessible by car or train from nearby towns like Gstaad and Montreux. Consider purchasing a Multi Pass for full access to activities and transportation.
- **Gear Up:** Dress for cold temperatures and changing weather conditions, even in summer. Bring sunscreen, sunglasses, and a hat for sunny days.
- **Timing Matters:** Peak season can get crowded, so consider visiting during weekdays or the shoulder seasons for a more serene experience.
- **Embrace the Unexpected:** Be prepared for the occasional change in weather, as mountain conditions can shift quickly.

Pack your sense of adventure and flexibility.

Remember: Glacier 3000 is more than just a collection of activities; it's an invitation to connect with the raw beauty and exhilarating spirit of the Alps. Whether you're conquering the Peak Walk, feeling the icy grip of the glacier, or simply soaking in the panoramic vistas, you'll find yourself transported to a surreal world where every moment is an adventure. So, gear up, pack your sense of wonder, and prepare to be swept away by the magic of Glacier 3000!

Happy adventures!

4.4 Titlis Rotair Gondola: Soaring Above Lush Green Pastures

The Titlis Rotair Gondola beckons with a unique experience: a 360-degree journey to the top of Mount Titlis, offering unparalleled views of lush green pastures, snow-capped peaks, and the captivating panorama of the Swiss Alps. Prepare to be awestruck by the beauty unfolding beneath you as you rotate your way to the summit!

The Thrill of the Ride:

- **Rotating Gondola:** This world-first engineering marvel gently spins while ascending, ensuring you don't miss a single breathtaking view. Imagine emerald valleys morphing into snow-dusted peaks, all while comfortably seated within the glass-enclosed cabin.
- **Panoramic Vistas:** Witness the vastness of the Swiss landscape, from the rolling green hills of Engelberg to the majestic glaciers and peaks that pierce the sky. Capture

every angle of this postcard-perfect scenery as you rotate to the top.

- **Uninterrupted Views:** Unlike traditional gondolas, the Rotair offers unobstructed visibility, allowing you to fully immerse yourself in the grandeur of the mountains without any window frames getting in the way.

Beyond the Gondola:

- **Titlis Glacier Park:** Upon reaching the summit, explore the Titlis Glacier Park, a wonderland of snow and ice activities. Go glacier skiing, ride the Ice Flyer coaster, or simply marvel at the mesmerizing ice caves.
- **Cliff Walk:** For the bold adventurers, challenge yourself on the Titlis Cliff Walk, Europe's highest suspension bridge. Adrenaline will pump as you walk across the bridge suspended 500 meters above the ground, with breathtaking views of the glacier and valley below.
- **Revolving Restaurant:** Indulge in a unique dining experience at the Rotair restaurant. Savor delicious Swiss cuisine while the panoramic views rotate around you, offering a constantly changing visual feast to accompany your meal.

Planning Your Ascent:

- **Location:** Easily accessible from Engelberg in central Switzerland. Purchase tickets online in advance, especially during peak season.
- **Gear Up:** Dress for varying weather conditions, as mountain temperatures can change quickly. Wear comfortable shoes suitable for walking on uneven terrain.

- **Timing is Key:** Aim for clear skies to maximize your viewing experience. Consider weekday visits for a less crowded gondola ride.
- **Embrace the Rotation:** Relax and enjoy the unique experience of the rotating gondola. Don't forget to capture every angle of the breathtaking scenery!

Remember: The Titlis Rotair Gondola is more than just a transportation – it's an adventure in itself. Prepare to be mesmerized by the 360-degree views, feel the thrill of the rotating cabin, and create memories that will forever be etched in your mind. So, buckle up, take a deep breath of fresh mountain air, and let the Rotair whisk you away to the heart of the Swiss Alps!

Happy soaring adventures!

5

Lakeside Trails and Hidden Gems: Discovering Enchanting Landscapes

Beyond the majestic peaks and sky-high cable cars, the Swiss landscape unveils a hidden dimension: its shimmering lakes and enchanting trails. Here, tranquility mingles with adventure, offering serene strolls beside turquoise waters and thrilling hikes through mystical forests. Let's embark on a journey to discover some of these captivating lakeside gems:

For the Serenity Seekers:

- **Oeschinen Lake:** Nestled amidst emerald mountains, Oeschinen Lake reflects the sky like a flawless mirror. Hike the idyllic shoreline trail, rent a pedal boat, or simply soak in the tranquility from a lakeside cafe.
- **Lake Lungern:** Embark on a scenic boat ride on Lake Lungern, marveling at the dramatic rock formations and hidden waterfalls. Hike to the nearby Melchsee for a secluded alpine haven.
- **Lake Lauenen:** Tucked away in the Bernese Oberland, Lauenen Lake offers a pristine escape. Hike through fragrant

pine forests, picnic on the grassy shores, or cast a line for some fresh mountain trout.

For the Adventure Enthusiasts:

- **Brienzersee:** Hike the challenging Brienzergrat ridge, enjoying panoramic views of the lake and surrounding peaks. For a unique perspective, kayak across the glassy surface or conquer the thrilling Axalphorn via ferrata.
- **Lake Thun:** Cycle the scenic Thun Panoramaweg, weaving through charming villages and vineyards. Take a cable car to the Niesen peak for breathtaking lake and mountain vistas.
- **Blausee:** Hike through verdant forests to reach the mystical Blausee, its waters shimmering with an otherworldly blue hue. Legend whispers of mythical creatures, adding to the enchanting atmosphere.

Beyond the Trails:

- **Discover charming lakeside villages:** Explore the quaint streets of Brienz, savor local cheeses in Gruyeres, or delve into the historical village of Interlaken.
- **Unwind in thermal baths:** Relax in the warm waters of the Leukerbad thermal springs, surrounded by breathtaking mountain scenery.
- **Embark on a scenic boat cruise:** Sail across Lake Geneva, admiring the grandeur of Lausanne and Montreux, or witness the majestic scenery of Lake Lucerne.

Planning Your Lakeside Escape:

- **Choose your region:** From the Bernese Oberland to the Swiss Riviera, each lake offers a unique atmosphere and activities.
- **Consider your fitness level:** Choose trails that match your abilities, from relaxing strolls to challenging hikes.
- **Pack for all weather conditions:** Mountain weather can change quickly, so be prepared for sunshine, rain, and even snow.
- **Respect the environment:** Leave no trace, minimize your impact on the delicate lakeside ecosystem, and enjoy the beauty responsibly.

Remember: The Swiss lakes are more than just scenic backdrops; they are vibrant ecosystems and enchanting escapes. By immersing yourself in their tranquility, embracing the adventure opportunities, and respecting their natural beauty, you'll create memories that will shimmer long after your journey ends.

So, lace up your boots, grab your swimsuit, and prepare to be captivated by the magic of the Swiss lakeside trails and hidden gems. Happy exploring!

5.1 Lake Oeschinen: Emerald Waters and Alpine Charm

Oeschinen Lake! Nestled amidst emerald mountains like a precious jewel, it's no wonder this alpine beauty captivates travelers from all corners of the globe. Prepare to be enchanted by its crystal-clear waters, lush meadows, and the invigorating spirit of the Swiss Alps.

A Landscape Painted in Emerald:

- **Mirror, Mirror on the Lake:** Witness the sky and surrounding peaks perfectly reflected in the still waters of Oeschinen See, creating a scene of breathtaking serenity.
- **Hiking Haven:** Lace up your boots and explore a network of trails that hug the shoreline, offering panoramic vistas at every turn. Choose from gentle strolls to challenging climbs, each revealing the lake's ever-changing beauty.
- **Emerald Embrace:** Lush meadows carpeted with wildflowers tumble down to the water's edge, inviting you to picnic, sunbathe, or simply soak in the tranquility of the alpine landscape.

Adventures on and off the Water:

- **Pedal Power:** Rent a pedal boat and glide across the glassy surface, feeling the cool mountain breeze against your skin as you admire the scenery from a unique perspective.
- **Fishing Fun:** Cast a line for arctic char and lake trout, thriving in the pristine waters of Oeschinen See. Enjoy the thrill of the catch and savor the fresh taste of a mountain delicacy.
- **Winter Wonderland:** When snow blankets the landscape, Oeschinen transforms into a winter wonderland. Go ice skating on the frozen lake, embark on a cross-country skiing adventure, or simply build a snowman and revel in the magical atmosphere.

Beyond the Lakeside Charm:

- **Kandersteg Calling:** Nestled just a short walk away, the charming village of Kandersteg offers a taste of Swiss culture. Explore its alpine architecture, indulge in local cheese and chocolate, and discover hidden waterfalls in the nearby forests.

- **Oeschinenbahn Gondola Ride:** For a bird's-eye view of the lake and surrounding mountains, take a scenic gondola ride to the top of Heuberg. The panoramic vistas will leave you breathless.
- **Thrill Seekers Welcome:** If you crave adrenaline, conquer the challenging Kander Gorge via ferrata, a network of ladders and cables scaling the dramatic rock face.

Planning Your Oeschinen Escape:

- **Accessibility:** Easily accessible by train and bus from major Swiss cities. Consider purchasing a Kandersteg Guest Card for discounted travel and activities.
- **Seasonal Delights:** Spring and summer offer warm weather and vibrant landscapes, while winter brings a fairytale atmosphere for snow enthusiasts.
- **Accommodation Options:** Choose from cozy guesthouses in Kandersteg to comfortable hotels near the lake, depending on your desired level of seclusion and amenities.
- **Respect the Gem:** Oeschinen See is a fragile ecosystem. Be a responsible visitor by following local regulations, disposing of waste properly, and minimizing your impact on the environment.

Remember: Oeschinen Lake is not just a scenic destination; it's an invitation to connect with the beauty and spirit of the Swiss Alps. Whether you seek serene hikes, refreshing dips, or winter wonderland adventures, Oeschinen promises to leave you enchanted and rejuvenated. So, pack your sense of adventure, embrace the emerald allure, and let Oeschinen Lake weave its magic on your soul.

Happy exploring!

5.2 Aare Gorge: Hiking Through a Natural Canyon Wonder

Prepare to be awestruck by the mighty Aare Gorge, a natural wonder carved by the churning Aare River through limestone cliffs for millennia. This dramatic canyon promises an unforgettable hiking experience, where towering rock walls whisper ancient tales and the roar of the water echoes through the air.

Stepping into a Geological Masterpiece:

- **Carved with Time:** Marvel at the awe-inspiring power of nature as you navigate narrow walkways and tunnels built into the sheer rock face. Imagine the millennia it took for the rushing Aare to sculpt this dramatic masterpiece.
- **Icy Embrace:** Feel the invigorating spray of the Aare River as it plummets past you, its turquoise waters glistening in the sunlight. The cool canyon air provides a refreshing escape from the summer heat.
- **Natural Playground:** Discover hidden waterfalls trickling down moss-covered walls, spot playful fish darting through the icy current, and witness the dance of butterflies flitting among wildflowers clinging to the rocks.

Adventure Awaits at Every Turn:

- **Walk into History:** Step back in time as you explore the historical tunnels and bridges, remnants of an old train line that once traversed the gorge. Imagine the chugging locomotives and the echoes of travelers from a bygone era.

- **Thrill Seekers Welcome:** For those craving a bit more adrenaline, try the high-ropes course suspended above the roaring river. Test your balance and courage as you swing through the air, enjoying breathtaking views from a unique perspective.
- **Family Fun for All:** The Aare Gorge offers trails suitable for all ages and fitness levels. Let the kids loose on the playground near the western entrance, while parents relax on a terrace overlooking the dramatic scenery.

Beyond the Canyon Walls:

- **Charming Meiringen:** Explore the charming village of Meiringen, known for its Sherlock Holmes Museum and traditional Swiss architecture. Indulge in local cheeses and chocolates, and soak in the laid-back atmosphere.
- **Reichenbach Falls:** Discover the enchanting Reichenbach Falls, cascading down a series of cliffs near Meiringen. Legend has it that this is where Sherlock Holmes met his demise at the hands of Professor Moriarty.
- **Rosenlaui Glacier Gorge:** Embark on another stunning hike through the Rosenlaui Glacier Gorge, accessible by cable car. Witness the power of glacial erosion and marvel at the pristine alpine scenery.

Planning Your Canyon Adventure:

- **Accessibility:** Easily accessible by train and bus from major

Swiss cities. The two entrances to the gorge are connected by a public walkway, offering a circular hike option.

- **Gear Up:** Wear comfortable shoes with good grip, as the pathways can be wet and slippery. Bring sunscreen and a hat for sunny days, and a rain jacket for unpredictable weather.
- **Timing Matters:** Weekends and summer months tend to be more crowded. Visit during weekdays or shoulder seasons for a more peaceful experience.
- **Responsible Exploration:** Respect the fragile ecosystem of the canyon. Dispose of waste properly, stick to designated paths, and minimize your impact on the environment.

Remember: The Aare Gorge is not just a hike; it's an immersive experience in the raw power and beauty of nature. Let the canyon walls embrace you, feel the spray of the Aare River refresh your soul, and create memories that will echo through your heart long after your visit.

So, lace up your boots, grab your sense of wonder, and prepare to be awestruck by the Aare Gorge! Happy hiking!

5.3 Lauterbrunnen Valley: Waterfalls, Villages, and Scenic Splendor

Prepare to be swept away by the magic of the Lauterbrunnen Valley, a spellbinding tapestry of cascading waterfalls, charming villages, and breathtaking panoramas nestled amidst the grandeur of the Swiss Alps. This verdant valley promises an unforgettable escape, where every turn unveils a new wonder and the symphony of rushing water washes away all your worries.

A Symphony of Waterfalls:

- **72 Natural Wonders:** Hike amidst the valley's claim to fame - 72 thundering waterfalls that cascade down lush cliffs, each one more mesmerizing than the last. Feel the invigorating spray of Staubbach Fall, marvel at the hidden power of Trümmelbach Falls, and discover the secret beauty of countless secluded cascades.
- **Waterfall Chasing Adventures:** Embark on an epic waterfall hunt, following well-marked trails or venturing off the beaten path to uncover hidden gems. Capture the power and grace of these watery wonders in photographs that will forever evoke the valley's magic.
- **Behind the Falls:** Delve into the heart of the action with a visit to the Trümmelbach Falls. Ride a funicular railway into the mountain and explore a series of subterranean walkways and tunnels, witnessing the hidden power of these majestic cascades from behind the scenes.

Village Charm and Alpine Delights:

- **Lauterbrunnen Jewel:** Nestled beneath Staubbach Fall, the village of Lauterbrunnen offers a delightful base for your valley adventures. Explore its charming streets lined with traditional chalets, browse local shops bursting with Swiss souvenirs, and savor delicious cheese fondue in a cozy mountain restaurant.
- **Wengen's Car-Free Paradise:** Take a car-free cogwheel train ride up to the idyllic village of Wengen, a haven of tranquility and scenic beauty. Wander through flower-filled meadows, enjoy breathtaking views of the Jungfrau massif,

and experience the authentic charm of Swiss mountain life.

- **Gimmelwald's Secluded Enchantment:** For a true escape, venture further up the valley to the tiny village of Gimmelwald. Accessible only by cable car or a scenic mountain footpath, it offers breathtaking panoramas, serene meadows, and a sense of timeless peace.

Beyond the Valley Floor:

- **Jungfraujoch – Top of Europe:** Ascend to the dizzying heights of the Jungfraujoch, Europe's highest railway station. Witness breathtaking alpine vistas, explore glacial ice caves, and experience the exhilaration of standing atop the continent.
- **Männlichen Mountain Panorama:** Take a cable car ride to the top of Männlichen Mountain and embark on a scenic hike along the Panoramaweg. Soak in panoramic views of the valley, surrounding peaks, and the glistening waters of Lake Brienz.
- **Schilthorn – Piz Gloria:** Embark on a James Bond-themed adventure with a trip to the Schilthorn. Take a revolving cable car ride to the Piz Gloria restaurant, made famous in the film "On Her Majesty's Secret Service," and enjoy breathtaking 360-degree views.

Planning Your Lauterbrunnen Escape:

- **Accessibility:** Easily accessible by train from major Swiss cities. Consider purchasing a regional travel pass for convenient and affordable transportation within the valley and surrounding areas.

- **Seasonal Delights:** Spring and summer offer vibrant landscapes and warm weather, while winter transforms the valley into a fairytale wonderland with snowy panoramas and festive cheer.
- **Accommodation Options:** Choose from charming guesthouses in Lauterbrunnen and Wengen to comfortable hotels with breathtaking views. For a truly unique experience, consider staying in a traditional alpine chalet.
- **Embrace the Spirit:** The Lauterbrunnen Valley is an invitation to slow down, connect with nature, and savor the simple pleasures of alpine life. Leave your worries behind, listen to the symphony of waterfalls, and create memories that will forever resonate in your soul.

Remember: The Lauterbrunnen Valley is not just a destination; it's an experience. Let its waterfalls serenade you, its villages charm you, and its panoramas mesmerize you. So, pack your sense of wonder, lace up your hiking boots, and prepare to be enchanted by the magic of this alpine paradise.

Happy adventures!

5.4 Melchsee Gondola: A Panoramic Paradise Above Engelberg

Nestled amidst the emerald embrace of the Bernese Oberland, the Melchsee Gondola beckons you on a captivating journey to a hidden Alpine paradise. Prepare to ascend above the charming village of Engelberg, leaving behind the bustling world and entering a realm of panoramic vistas, serene lakes, and a sense of timeless tranquility.

Soaring to New Heights:

- **Gondola Glide:** Embark on a scenic gondola ride, gently ascending through alpine meadows and pine forests. Witness the dramatic transformation of the landscape as Engelberg shrinks below, and breathtaking peaks pierce the sky.
- **Panoramic Unveiling:** As you reach the summit, a breathtaking panorama unfolds before your eyes. Lush valleys dotted with wildflowers carpet the hills, shimmering lakes reflect the azure sky, and the majestic peaks of Titlis and Sustenhorn stand sentinel against the horizon.
- **Fresh Mountain Air:** Breathe in the crisp, invigorating air, scented with pine needles and wildflowers. Feel the tension melt away as you immerse yourself in the tranquility of the mountain sanctuary.

A Playground for Every Soul:

- **Melchsee Magic:** Discover the enchanting Melchsee, a serene lake nestled amidst the mountain slopes. Paddle across its glassy surface, cast a line for its resident trout, or simply picnic on its shores and soak in the serene beauty.
- **Hiking Heaven:** Lace up your boots and explore a network of trails catering to all levels. Embark on gentle strolls around the lake, conquer challenging climbs to hidden viewpoints, or follow the historic Melchsee-Frutt Loop for a comprehensive exploration.
- **Family Fun:** Let the kids loose on the Melchsee-Frutt playground, equipped with slides, swings, and climbing structures. Enjoy a family picnic on the lush meadows, or build a sandcastle by the lake's edge.

Beyond the Gondola's Reach:

- **Engelberg Adventure:** Explore the charming village of Engelberg, a delightful base for your Alpine escapades. Visit the Benedictine monastery, browse local shops, or indulge in traditional Swiss cuisine in cozy restaurants.
- **Titlis Glacier Park:** For an extra dose of adrenaline, ascend to the top of Mount Titlis and experience the thrills of the glacier park. Ride the Ice Flyer coaster, go glacier skiing, or explore the mesmerizing ice caves.
- **Trübsee Treasure:** Hike or take a scenic chairlift to the tranquil Trübsee lake, nestled amidst towering peaks. Enjoy water sports activities, savor a delicious meal at the lakeside restaurant, or simply relax and soak in the breathtaking scenery.

Planning Your Panoramic Escape:

- **Accessibility:** Easily accessible by train and bus from major Swiss cities. Purchase a gondola ticket or an Engelberg Visitor Card for additional discounts and activities.
- **Seasonal Delights:** Spring and summer offer vibrant landscapes and warm weather, while winter transforms the area into a wonderland for skiers and snowboarders.
- **Gear Up:** Dress for varying weather conditions, as mountain temperatures can change quickly. Wear comfortable shoes suitable for hiking or walking on uneven terrain.
- **Embrace the Moment:** Slow down, disconnect from the digital world, and immerse yourself in the beauty of the surrounding nature. Savor the silence, listen to the chirping of birds, and create memories that will last a lifetime.

Remember: The Melchsee Gondola is more than just a trans-portation device; it's a gateway to a world of Alpine enchant-ment. Let the panoramic vistas captivate you, the mountain air invigorate you, and the serene beauty of Melchsee lake touch your soul. So, pack your sense of wonder, grab your camera, and prepare to be swept away by the magic of this breathtaking paradise above Engelberg.

Happy adventures!

6

Thematic Adventures: Tailoring Your Hike to Your Passions

Hike beyond the ordinary and tap into your passions! Choose a trail that resonates with your interests, offering an experience filled with excitement, discovery, and a touch of your personal flair. Here are some ideas to get you started:

For the History Buff:

- **Walk the Roman Roads:** Hike the Via Francigena, an ancient pilgrimage route dating back to the Roman Empire. Imagine the footsteps of emperors and pilgrims as you traverse charming villages and breathtaking landscapes.
- **Battlefields and Castles:** Follow in the footsteps of soldiers and explore historical battlefields like Marathon or Gettysburg. Hike to ancient castles like Neuschwanstein in Germany or Stirling Castle in Scotland, immersing yourself in medieval magic.
- **Lost Civilizations:** Trek the Inca Trail to Machu Picchu,

marvel at the ruins of Angkor Wat in Cambodia, or explore the mysteries of Tikal in Guatemala. Connect with forgotten civilizations and feel the weight of history in your steps.

For the Nature Lover:

- **Botanical Bonanza:** Embark on a wildflower hike through meadows bursting with vibrant blooms. Identify rare species, learn about medicinal plants, and capture the ephemeral beauty of nature's tapestry.
- **Glacial Giants:** Trek amidst awe-inspiring glaciers in Patagonia, New Zealand, or the Swiss Alps. Feel the power of ice, witness meltwater carving dramatic landscapes, and stand humbled by the Earth's ancient forces.
- **Waterfall Wonderland:** Chase waterfalls on the Isle of Skye in Scotland, hike to Victoria Falls in Africa, or navigate the mist-shrouded trails of Yosemite National Park. Feel the spray on your face, listen to the thunderous roar, and find hidden gems tucked away behind cascading waters.

For the Thrill Seeker:

- **Via Ferrata Adventures:** Test your courage and climb vertical rock faces with the aid of cables and ladders. Conquer iconic routes like the Caminito del Rey in Spain or the Grosse Scheidegg in Switzerland, and savor the panoramic rewards.
- **Canyoning Delights:** Plunge into refreshing canyons, rappel down waterfalls, and slide through natural waterslides. Explore hidden gorges in Utah's Zion National Park, navigate the rugged terrain of Madeira Island, or discover the dramatic canyons of Arizona.

- **Volcanic Escapes:** Hike active volcanoes in Guatemala, climb Mount Fuji in Japan, or trek through the geothermal wonderland of Iceland. Feel the earth's heat, witness the raw power of nature, and create memories that will forever crackle with excitement.

For the Culture Enthusiast:

- **Food and Wine Trails:** Hike through vineyards in Italy's Tuscany, discover hidden rice paddies in Bali, or wander through spice plantations in Kerala, India. Learn about local customs, savor regional delicacies, and connect with the land through its culinary heritage.
- **Ancient Trails and Traditions:** Walk the El Camino de Santiago in Spain, explore the Great Wall of China, or trek the Inca Trail to Machu Picchu. Immerse yourself in ancient traditions, connect with diverse cultures, and learn about their profound relationship with the land.
- **Tribal Trails:** Join guided treks led by indigenous communities in the Amazon rainforest, the Australian Outback, or the Mongolian steppes. Learn about their traditional way of life, respect their connection to the land, and discover hidden corners of the world through their eyes.

Remember: These are just a few ideas to spark your imagination. With a little creativity, you can tailor any hike to your passions, turning it into an adventure that resonates with your soul. So, lace up your boots, grab your backpack, and prepare to embark on a thematic journey that will leave you breathless, inspired, and forever connected to the wonders of the world!

Happy trails!

6.1 Historical Hike: Retracing the Footsteps of William Tell

Immerse yourself in Swiss legend and history with a hike retracing the footsteps of the iconic crossbow marksman, William Tell. This adventure winds through scenic landscapes and charming villages, blending breathtaking panoramas with tales of heroism and rebellion.

The Call to Adventure:

- **Uri Canton Charm:** Begin your journey in the canton of Uri, nestled amidst the heart of the Swiss Alps. Explore the picturesque town of Brunnen, where legend has it Tell shot the apple off his son's head, and feel the spirit of resistance reverberate through the cobbled streets.
- **Rütli Meadow - Cradle of Freedom:** Hike alongside the shores of Lake Lucerne to the Rütli Meadow, a symbol of Swiss independence. Imagine the oath sworn by Tell and his compatriots, sparking the flames of revolution against Habsburg rule.
- **Tellskapelle - A Sanctuary of Legend:** Visit the Tellskapelle, a small chapel perched on a rocky outcrop overlooking the lake. Witness the murals depicting Tell's exploits and soak in the serene atmosphere, where legend and history seem to intertwine.

Walking Among Legends:

- **Axenstrasse Hike:** Embark on a scenic trail along the Axenstrasse, a historic road carved into the cliffs above Lake Lucerne. Witness breathtaking views of the surrounding peaks and imagine the treacherous journey Tell undertook to escape his captors.

- **Bauen - Traces of the Past:** Explore the charming village of Bauen, where Tell is said to have leaped from a boat to freedom. Visit the Tell Museum and delve deeper into the legend, imagining the courage and resilience of the folk hero.
- **Gesslerburg Ruins:** Hike to the ruins of Gesslerburg, the former seat of the tyrannical governor against whom Tell rebelled. Stand amidst the crumbling walls and feel the echoes of a bygone era, where power struggles shaped the destiny of this nation.

Beyond the Legend:

- **Brunnen Boat Cruise:** Sail across Lake Lucerne, enjoying panoramic views of the surrounding mountains and charming villages. Imagine Tell navigating these waters during his daring escape, adding a touch of historical perspective to your scenic journey.
- **Ruetli Meadow Festival:** If planning your trip for August, coincide it with the Rütli Meadow Festival, a vibrant celebration of Swiss unity and tradition. Witness colorful parades, folk music performances, and traditional costume displays, immersing yourself in the living spirit of the legend.
- **Swiss Chocolate Delights:** Indulge in a uniquely Swiss experience by visiting a local chocolate factory or indulging in decadent treats at a cozy cafe. Savor the rich flavors and appreciate the craftsmanship that defines this national treasure.

Planning Your Footsteps of Tell Adventure:

- **Accessibility:** Easily accessible by train and bus from major Swiss cities. Consider purchasing a regional travel pass for convenient and affordable transportation within the canton of Uri.
- **Seasonal Delights:** Spring and summer offer warm weather and vibrant landscapes, while winter transforms the area into a wonderland for winter sports enthusiasts.
- **Gear Up:** Dress for varying weather conditions and comfortable shoes suitable for hiking trails. Bring sunscreen, a hat, and water, especially during warmer months.
- **Embrace the Legend:** Let the stories of William Tell come alive as you retrace his steps. Imagine the sights, sounds, and emotions of the era, adding a layer of historical richness to your hike.

Remember: This hike is not just about retracing footsteps; it's about celebrating the spirit of independence, courage, and unity that defines Switzerland. So, step into the legend of William Tell, listen to the whispers of history, and create memories that will echo through your own journey of exploration.

Happy trails!

6.2 Culinary Hike: Delectable Discoveries at Mountain Huts

Embark on a flavor-filled adventure with a culinary hike, savoring the unique and delectable delights offered by traditional Swiss mountain huts. This journey isn't just about conquering peaks; it's about tantalizing your taste buds with fresh, local ingredients and rustic charm, where every bite tells a story of the mountains and their people.

A Feast for the Senses:

- **Alpine Gastronomy:** Immerse yourself in the warmth and aroma of a cozy mountain hut, its wood-paneled walls and crackling fireplace setting the perfect scene for culinary indulgence. Sample hearty dishes like cheese fondue, raclette, and rösti potatoes, each bite bursting with the flavor of alpine meadows and local craftsmanship.
- **Fresh Flavors from the Farm:** Savor the taste of authenticity with dishes featuring ingredients sourced from nearby farms and pastures. Imagine the sweetness of locally-made cheese, the earthy taste of wild mushrooms, and the juicy tenderness of mountain-raised lamb, all woven into mouthwatering creations.
- **Liquid Gold of the Alps:** Pair your meal with a glass of invigorating Swiss cider or a smooth local beer, crafted with pure mountain water and time-honored brewing traditions. Let the crisp flavors complement your food and elevate the dining experience to a celebration of regional heritage.

Hiking with a Fork:

- **Grindelwald to First: Cheese Heaven:** Tackle the challenging yet rewarding Faulhorn trail from Grindelwald to First, conquering steep inclines and breathtaking panoramas. Reward your efforts with a hearty cheese fondue at the First Mountain Resort, surrounded by breathtaking views of the Jungfrau massif.
- **Engelberg to Trübsee: Sweet Indulgence:** Embark on a picturesque hike from Engelberg to the idyllic Trübsee lake. Refuel at the Gaferei Restaurant, renowned for its melt-in-your-mouth meringues and cream cakes, savoring the delicate sweetness under the summer sun.
- **Zermatt to Schwarzsee: A Taste of History:** Hike through the dramatic landscape of Zermatt, passing alpine meadows and glistening glaciers. Reach the Schwarzsee lake and settle in at the Hotel Schwarzsee, a historic mountain hut serving traditional dishes like venison stew and roasted potatoes, cooked in wood-fired ovens.

Beyond the Huts:

- **Local Farmer's Markets:** Discover the bounty of the region at bustling farmer's markets, bursting with fresh fruits, vegetables, and artisanal cheeses. Pick up picnic supplies for an impromptu feast amidst the mountains, savoring the simple pleasures of local produce.
- **Charming Village Delights:** Explore charming villages nestled at the foot of the peaks. Discover hidden bakeries offering crusty breads and flaky pastries, cheese shops overflowing with pungent delights, and chocolatiers tempting you with their irresistible creations.
- **Cooking Classes at a Hut:** Immerse yourself fully in the

alpine culinary tradition by participating in a cooking class at a mountain hut. Learn the secrets of local recipes, master the art of cheese fondue, and create memories that will forever linger on your palate.

Planning Your Culinary Hike:

- **Accessibility:** Many mountain huts are accessible by hiking trails, cable cars, or a combination of both. Choose a route that matches your fitness level and desired level of challenge.
- **Reservations Recommended:** Popular huts often fill up quickly, especially during peak season. Book your table in advance to ensure you don't miss out on the delectable bounty.
- **Cash is King:** Many mountain huts are cash-only, so plan accordingly and bring enough Swiss francs to cover your meal and drinks.
- **Respect the Environment:** Leave no trace and dispose of your waste responsibly, ensuring that the beauty of the mountains and the deliciousness of their culinary heritage are preserved for future generations.

Remember: This hike is an invitation to connect with the soul of Switzerland through its flavors. Savor every bite, appreciate the warmth of the mountain hospitality, and create memories that will nourish your body and soul long after you've descended from the peaks.

Happy feasting and hiking!

6.3 Scenic Train and Hike: Combining Hiking with Panoramic Journeys

Embark on an adventure that seamlessly blends panoramic train journeys with invigorating hikes, offering the best of both worlds: breathtaking landscapes unfolding from your window and the thrill of conquering trails nestled amidst them. This is the perfect way to experience the grandeur of Switzerland, combining comfort and challenge, awe-inspiring vistas and earthy exploration.

A Symphony of Sights and Steps:

- **Glacier Express Panorama:** Glide through a wonderland of glacial ice and alpine majesty aboard the legendary Glacier Express. Witness the glistening peaks of the Jungfraujoch, traverse dramatic gorges, and marvel at cascading waterfalls, all from the comfort of your panoramic carriage.
- **Charming Village Stops:** Disembark at quaint villages along the route and stretch your legs with short hikes. Explore vibrant alpine meadows, discover hidden waterfalls, and savor local delicacies in mountain restaurants, adding a touch of human connection to your scenic journey.
- **Trailhead Connections:** Alight at strategically located train stations that serve as gateways to iconic hiking trails. From the Jungfraujoch, conquer challenging climbs to mountain summits, while charming Lauterbrunnen offers access to a network of trails leading to glistening waterfalls and serene alpine lakes.

Hike and Ride Your Way Through Swiss Landscapes:

- **Bernina Express and Piz Palü Hike:** Ride the Bernina Express through dramatic mountain passes and spiral tunnels, then embark on a breathtaking hike to the Piz Palü viewpoint. Witness panoramic vistas of glaciers, valleys, and shimmering lakes, feeling the exhilaration of conquering the ascent.
- **GoldenPass Panoramic Hike:** Journey through fairytale landscapes aboard the GoldenPass train, traversing rolling hills, lush vineyards, and picturesque villages. Step off at Gstaad and hike through pristine meadows, reaching a secluded alpine lake for a swim in its refreshing waters.
- **Furka Pass Steam Train and Trift Glacier Hike:** Experience the nostalgia of a vintage steam train ride on the Furka Pass. At Realp, embark on a challenging hike to the Trift Glacier, passing rugged landscapes and experiencing the raw power of glacial ice.

Beyond the Tracks and Trails:

- **Thermal Baths Rejuvenation:** After a day of hiking, soothe your muscles and indulge in relaxation at one of Switzerland's many thermal baths. Immerse yourself in warm, mineral-rich waters, surrounded by breathtaking alpine scenery.
- **Charming Village Delights:** Explore the quaint villages dotting the Swiss landscape. Wander through cobbled streets, browse local shops for souvenirs, and savor traditional dishes in cozy restaurants, soaking in the authentic charm of Alpine life.
- **Museum Immersions:** Immerse yourself in Swiss culture and history by visiting museums located near your train

journey or hiking routes. Discover fascinating exhibits on everything from chocolate making to mountaineering, adding depth and insight to your experiences.

Planning Your Scenic Train and Hike Adventure:

- **Choose Your Theme:** Select train journeys and hikes that resonate with your interests, whether it's chasing glaciers, conquering mountain peaks, or exploring charming villages.
- **Accessibility:** Consider your fitness level when choosing hikes and plan your train connections accordingly. Many trains offer luggage storage, making it easy to seamlessly transition between journeys.
- **Weather Matters:** Be prepared for changing weather conditions in the mountains. Pack layers, sturdy shoes, and rain gear, especially during spring and fall.
- **Embrace the Journey:** Don't rush. Savor the panoramic views from the train, enjoy the tranquility of the hikes, and appreciate the unique blend of comfort and challenge this adventure offers.

Remember: This scenic train and hike journey is not just about reaching destinations; it's about embracing the entire experience. Let the train whisk you through awe-inspiring landscapes, feel the earth beneath your feet as you conquer new terrain, and create memories that will forever connect you to the magic of Switzerland.

Happy trails and scenic rides!

6.4 Wellness Hike: Mindfulness and Breathtaking Views Along Yoga Trails

Breathe deeply, stretch towards the sun, and feel your cares melt away on a wellness hike designed to nourish your body, mind, and spirit. Immerse yourself in the beauty of Swiss mountains, but this time, not just as a spectator, but as an active participant in a holistic experience that blends physical movement, mindfulness, and stunning scenery.

Unfolding Your Inner Strength:

- **Yoga in the Alps:** Embrace the invigorating mountain air as you begin your day with a guided yoga session at the base of your chosen trail. Flow through postures designed to awaken your senses, connect with your breath, and prepare your body for the journey ahead.
- **Mindful Movement:** As you hike, focus on each step, feeling the connection between your breath, your movement, and the natural world around you. Notice the textures of the earth beneath your feet, the scent of pine trees, and the sound of birdsong.
- **Yoga Poses on Scenic Viewpoints:** Pause at breathtaking overlooks and integrate short yoga sequences that echo the surrounding landscape. Stretch your arms like soaring eagles, balance like mountain goats on sturdy rocks, and feel your connection to the vastness of nature.

Trails that Heal and Inspire:

- **Rigi Kaltbad - Rigi First: Embrace Serenity:** Hike amidst lush meadows and serene forests on the Rigi Kaltbad - Rigi

73

First trail. Practice sun salutations at sunrise on the Rigi Kulm summit, marveling at the panoramic views of Lake Lucerne and beyond.

- **Lauterbrunnen Valley - Trümmelbach Falls:** Find Inner Power:** Navigate the challenging ascent to the Trümmelbach Falls in the Lauterbrunnen Valley. Channel the power of the cascading water as you flow through warrior poses and balance exercises, feeling your own inner strength and resilience.
- **Lake Oeschinen - Kandersteg:** Connect with Nature:** Experience the vibrant emerald waters of Lake Oeschinen on a gentle trail near Kandersteg. Practice tree poses amidst the surrounding spruce forest, grounding yourself in the earth and finding peace amongst the natural beauty.

Beyond the Steps and Poses:

- **Meditation in Mountain Meadows:** Find a secluded meadow and settle into a guided meditation session. Let the sights and sounds of nature wash over you as you release stress and connect with your inner stillness.
- **Mindful Meals:** Savor your picnic lunch by the lake or a post-hike dinner at a mountain restaurant. Pay attention to each bite, appreciating the flavors and textures, and nourishing your body with intention.
- **Thermal Baths Rejuvenation:** After a day of mindful movement, melt away any remaining tension in the warm waters of a thermal bath. Float amidst the serene atmosphere, allowing the mineral-rich water to soothe your muscles and revitalize your spirit.

Planning Your Wellness Hike:

- **Accessibility:** Choose trails that match your fitness level and desired level of challenge. Most yoga trails incorporate accessible sections with optional challenging routes.
- **Gear Up:** Pack comfortable hiking shoes, layers of clothing suitable for changing weather, and a yoga mat or towel for your outdoor practice.
- **Open Your Mind:** This is a journey of self-discovery, not a fitness competition. Focus on your inner experience, embrace the present moment, and enjoy the process of connecting with your body, mind, and the natural world.
- **Leave No Trace:** Respect the fragile ecosystems of the mountains. Pack out all your trash and be mindful of your impact on the environment.

Remember: This wellness hike is an invitation to move beyond the ordinary and into a mindful dance with your own well-being. Breathe deeply, move with intention, and let the breathtaking scenery of Switzerland nourish your soul. You'll return from this journey feeling stronger, more connected, and deeply rejuvenated.

Happy trails and peaceful moments!

III

Essential Tips and Safety Guidelines

The Swiss Alps, with their majestic peaks, emerald valleys, and crystal-clear lakes, are a hiker's paradise. But before you embark on your Alpine adventure, it's crucial to be prepared and prioritize safety. Here are some essential tips and guidelines to ensure a memorable and worry-free journey

7

Hiking Etiquette and Mountain Respect: Sharing the Trails Responsibly

Conquering a mountain peak or traversing a scenic trail is an exhilarating experience, but it's important to remember that we share these natural treasures with fellow adventurers and the delicate alpine ecosystem. So, let's lace up our boots with a heart full of respect and embrace responsible hiking etiquette!

Sharing the Path:

- **Yield gracefully:** Uphill hikers have the right of way. Step aside and offer a friendly greeting as they ascend. Remember, you might be in their shoes soon!
- **Single file, please:** Unless passing, stick to single file on narrow trails. This keeps the flow smooth and helps avoid collisions.
- **Announce your presence:** When approaching blind corners or tight spots, announce yourself with a friendly "hello" or "coming through." Surprise encounters can lead to stumbles and scrapes.

Leave No Trace:

- **Pack it in, pack it out:** Carry all your trash, including banana peels and apple cores. Leave the mountains as pristine as you found them.
- **Minimize campfire impact:** If fires are allowed, use designated fire rings and extinguish them thoroughly with water and stir the ashes before leaving. Respect fire restrictions and regulations.
- **Stay on designated trails:** Sticking to marked trails helps protect fragile vegetation and prevents erosion. Remember, the off-trail allure can lead to unintended consequences.

Be a Mountain Steward:

- **Minimize noise:** Keep your music to yourself and avoid loud shouts. Let the symphony of nature be the soundtrack to your adventure.
- **Respect wildlife:** Observe animals from a distance and never feed them. This disrupts their natural behavior and can be harmful.
- **Be weather-wise:** Check the forecast before you go and be prepared for changing conditions. Dress in layers, pack essentials, and know your limits.

Building Community:

- **Offer a helping hand:** If you see someone struggling, offer assistance if it's safe to do so. A friendly word of encouragement can go a long way on the trail.
- **Celebrate shared moments:** A summit selfie or a shared

snack is a great way to connect with fellow hikers. Spread the joy of the mountains and build camaraderie on the trail.

Remember: Mountains are majestic yet fragile, demanding respect and care. By embracing these simple etiquette tips, we can ensure a safe and enjoyable experience for everyone, while preserving the magic of these natural wonders for generations to come. Let's leave only footprints, take only memories, and share the love for the mountains responsibly!

Happy trails, filled with respect and joy!

7.1 Leave No Trace Principles: Minimizing Your Impact on Nature

Exploring the beauty of nature is a transformative experience, but with great exploration comes great responsibility. Embracing the Leave No Trace principles ensures you enjoy your wilderness adventures while safeguarding the natural world for future generations. So, let's unpack these seven essential principles and see how we can all be responsible stewards of the outdoors.

1. Plan Ahead and Prepare:

- **Know before you go:** Research weather conditions, terrain, and regulations for your chosen area. Choose a destination and activity that matches your skills and physical abilities.
- **Leave no trace from the start:** Pack all the gear and supplies you need to avoid relying on scavenging or taking resources from the environment.

2. Travel and Camp on Durable Surfaces:

- **Stick to designated trails:** This protects flora and fauna from trampling and allows them to thrive. Create memories instead of footprints.
- **Camp in established campsites:** Minimize soil disturbance and avoid sensitive areas like meadows or riverbanks. Leave the campsite better than you found it.

3. Dispose of Waste Properly:

- **Pack it in, pack it out:** Everything you bring in, even orange peels and banana cores, must leave with you. Leave no trace of your visit.
- **Minimize waste at the source:** Opt for reusable containers and water bottles, and choose biodegradable products when possible. Reduce what needs to be disposed of in the first place.

4. Leave What You Find:

- **Leave natural objects and artifacts untouched:** Leave rocks, plants, and historical relics undisturbed. Let others enjoy the natural beauty as you found it.
- **Minimize fire impacts:** If fires are allowed, use designated fire rings and extinguish them completely before leaving. Respect fire restrictions and regulations.

5. Minimize Campfire Impacts:

- **Choose a fire-safe location:** Avoid flammable vegetation or areas prone to strong winds. Leave the ground free of debris and create a fire ring from rocks if one isn't already present.

- **Use dead and down wood:** Never cut down healthy trees or living branches for firewood. Respect the lifeblood of the forest.

6. Respect Wildlife:

- **Observe wildlife from a distance:** This minimizes interference with their natural behavior and protects them from stress. Never approach or feed wild animals.
- **Store food and trash securely:** Use bear canisters or hang food bags away from campsites to avoid attracting curious creatures and potential conflicts.

7. Be Considerate of Other Visitors:

- **Yield to uphill traffic:** Let hikers ascending the trail have the right of way. A simple "hello" or a step aside goes a long way in sharing the trail.
- **Minimize noise:** Keep your music to yourself and avoid loud shouts. Let the sounds of nature be the soundtrack to everyone's experience.

Remember: Each of us has the power to leave a positive or negative impact on the environment. By embracing the Leave No Trace principles, we can protect the delicate balance of nature and ensure our wild spaces remain pristine for generations to come. Let's explore with responsibility, celebrate the beauty of the natural world, and leave only footprints of respect and care.

Happy trails, filled with mindful exploration and respect for nature!

7.2 Respecting Local Traditions and Wildlife Encounters

Venturing into new landscapes isn't just about conquering peaks and soaking in vistas; it's about immersing yourself in the cultural tapestry and respecting the delicate dance between humans and wildlife. So, let's lace up our boots with a heart full of cultural sensitivity and responsible wildlife etiquette!

Honoring Local Traditions:

- **Dress appropriately:** Be mindful of local customs and dress modestly when visiting religious sites or villages with specific dress codes. Avoid revealing clothing that might cause offense.
- **Ask before you photograph:** Not everyone enjoys having their picture taken. Always seek permission before capturing portraits, especially of individuals or sensitive religious sites.
- **Support local communities:** Choose to stay in locally-owned homestays, eat at family-run restaurants, and purchase souvenirs from craftspeople. Your tourism dollars can bring positive change.
- **Learn basic greetings:** A few words in the local language go a long way. "Hello," "Thank you," and "Please" show respect and open doors to friendly interactions.
- **Respect sacred spaces:** Be mindful of religious sites and customs. Dress modestly, maintain silence in designated areas, and avoid disruptive behavior.

Encounters with Wildlife:

- **Observe from a distance:** Never approach or try to touch wild animals. This disrupts their natural behavior and can be dangerous for both you and them.
- **Avoid making loud noises:** Keep your voice low and avoid sudden movements that might startle wildlife. Let them enjoy their habitat without human interference.
- **Do not feed wildlife:** This creates dependence and can lure animals into conflict zones with humans. Never offer human food or scraps, stick to their natural diet.
- **Pack out all trash:** Food scraps and plastic bags can attract and harm wildlife. Ensure you clean up after yourself and leave no trace of your visit.
- **Report unusual behavior:** If you witness injured or aggressive animals, report the situation to park rangers or local authorities. Early intervention can prevent harm to both humans and wildlife.

Remember: We are guests in these breathtaking landscapes, sharing them with diverse cultures and fascinating creatures. By embracing respectful behavior and cultural sensitivity, we can minimize our impact, foster genuine connections with local communities, and ensure the well-being of wildlife. Let's explore with open hearts and open minds, leaving behind only footprints of appreciation and a legacy of responsible interaction.

Happy trails, filled with cultural sensitivity and wildlife respect!

7.3 Staying Safe on the Mountain: Weather Awareness and Emergency Tips

Conquering a mountain peak or traversing a serene trail is an exhilarating experience, but amidst the breathtaking landscapes lies an inherent responsibility – ensuring your own safety and well-being. By prioritizing weather awareness and equipping yourself with essential emergency tips, you can turn your mountain adventure into a story of resilience and responsible exploration.

Weather Wisdom:

- **Check the forecast before you go:** This isn't just a suggestion; it's a mandatory first step. Research expected conditions, including temperature, wind speed, precipitation, and potential storms.
- **Dress in layers:** Be prepared for rapid weather changes. Wear breathable base layers, insulating mid-layers, and a waterproof outer shell to adapt to fluctuating temperatures and unexpected rain or snow.
- **Mind the wind chill:** Wind can dramatically decrease the perceived temperature, making you feel colder than the thermometer actually reads. Factor in wind chill when choosing your clothing and packing additional layers.
- **Know your limits:** Don't underestimate the severity of mountain weather. If conditions seem beyond your experience or comfort level, don't hesitate to turn back. Your safety is paramount.
- **Stay informed:** Monitor weather updates throughout your hike. Utilize weather apps, listen to local radio broadcasts, and stay in touch with park rangers or guides for the latest

developments.

Emergency Preparedness:

- **Pack smart:** Carry a well-stocked backpack with essentials like a map, compass, GPS device (with downloaded maps), first-aid kit, emergency shelter (space blanket or bivy sack), headlamp, fire starter, whistle, and extra food and water.
- **Tell someone your plans:** Share your route and expected return time with a trusted friend or family member. Inform them of any changes in your plans and check in periodically.
- **Learn basic navigation:** Knowing how to read a map and compass is crucial if technology fails. Consider taking a navigation course before venturing into unfamiliar terrain.
- **Stay hydrated and fueled:** Dehydration and exhaustion can impair your judgment and increase risks. Pack ample water and high-energy snacks, and make sure to replenish fluids and calories regularly throughout your hike.
- **Be prepared for the unexpected:** Accidents happen, even to experienced hikers. Pack a first-aid kit and know basic first-aid procedures. If you encounter an injured person, stay calm and call for help immediately.

Remember: Mountains are awe-inspiring, but they can also be unpredictable and unforgiving. By prioritizing weather awareness, packing essential gear, and being prepared for emergencies, you turn your mountain adventure into a story of responsible exploration and resilience. Let breathtaking vistas be paired with the assurance of safety, knowing you've taken the necessary steps to navigate the challenges and emerge with unforgettable memories.

Happy trails, filled with mindful planning and safe adventures!

8

Conclusion

Glossary of Terms: Understanding Swiss Hiking Lingo

Gearing up for a Swiss hiking adventure? Hold on to your crampons, because understanding the local lingo can add a whole new layer of enjoyment to your journey. Here's a handy glossary to navigate the trails with confidence:

The Terrain:

- **Alpe:** A high-altitude pasture, often used for grazing cattle. Imagine lush meadows carpeted with wildflowers, with the scent of fresh milk and cheese in the air.
- **Grat:** A ridge or crest of a mountain. Picture yourself standing on a sharp edge, with breathtaking views on either side.
- **Gletscher:** A glacier, a majestic river of ice carved by time and nature. Respect its power and admire its beauty from a safe distance.
- **Kar:** A bowl-shaped valley formed by glacial erosion. Think

of a giant's scooped-out ice cream bowl, filled with stunning scenery.

· **Schlucht:** A gorge, a dramatic and narrow passage carved by water through rocks. Feel the coolness of the air and the thrill of being surrounded by towering cliffs.

The Trail Talk:

· **Bergführer:** A mountain guide, your expert companion on challenging routes. Trust their knowledge and enjoy a safe and informative trek.

· **Seilbahn:** A cable car or gondola, whisking you up to breathtaking heights in a comfortable ride. Let the panoramic views take your breath away.

· **Wanderweg:** A hiking trail, ranging from gentle nature walks to challenging mountain climbs. Choose your path and embrace the adventure.

· **Wegweiser:** A signpost, your friendly guide on the trail. Follow its directions and never get lost in the maze of mountain paths.

· **Zwiesel:** A fork in the path, a moment of decision. Choose wisely, or simply wander and discover hidden gems along the way.

Bonus Words:

· **Gemütlichkeit:** Cozy comfort and warmth, the feeling of being nestled by a crackling fire in a mountain hut after a long day on the trail.

· **Gipfelglück:** Summit happiness, the exhilarating feeling of reaching the top and soaking in the panoramic victory.

- **Wanderlust:** A love for wandering, the irresistible urge to explore new trails and embrace the beauty of the natural world.

Remember: This glossary is just a starting point. Don't be afraid to ask locals for help or clarification. Their friendly smiles and helpful directions will add another layer of charm to your Swiss hiking experience.

Happy trails and happy learning!

Useful Resources: Maps, Apps, and Local Information Links

Embarking on a Swiss hiking adventure requires preparation, and access to the right resources can make all the difference. Here's a curated list of maps, apps, and local information links to ensure a smooth and memorable journey:

Maps:

- **SwissTopo:** The official topographic map of Switzerland, offering incredible detail and accuracy. Choose printed maps or access the interactive online platform: https://www.swisstopo.admin.ch/de/karten-daten-online/karten-geodaten-online.html
- **SchweizMobil:** Provides an extensive network of hiking trails with downloadable maps and route planning tools: https://schweizmobil.ch/en/hiking-in-switzerland
- **Wanderland Schweiz:** An interactive online platform showcasing curated hiking routes with detailed descriptions, photos, and downloadable maps: https://schweizmobil.ch/en/winter

Apps:

- **SchweizMobil App:** Access the entire SchweizMobil network on your phone, including live track recording, offline maps, and points of interest: https://schweizmobil.ch/de/app-schweizmobil
- **SwissTopo App:** Offers detailed topographic maps on your phone, perfect for navigation and finding your way in remote areas: https://www.swisstopo.admin.ch/en/maps-data-online/maps-geodata-online/swisstopo-app.html
- **PeakFinder:** Identify surrounding peaks from your current location, enhancing your connection to the landscape: https://www.peakfinder.com/mobile/
- **SAC Schweiz:** Access information about mountain huts, weather conditions, and safety tips from the Swiss Alpine Club: https://www.sac-cas.ch/

Local Information Links:

- **MySwitzerland:** Switzerland's official tourism website, offering comprehensive information on hiking routes, transportation, accommodation, and more: https://www.myswitzerland.com/en/
- **Weather Switzerland:** Check the latest weather forecasts and warnings for your chosen region: https://www.meteoswiss.admin.ch/
- **Swiss Alpine Rescue:** Find emergency contact information and safety tips for alpine regions: https://www.rega.ch/en/
- **Local tourism websites:** Most towns and villages have their own tourism websites with specific information about hiking trails, events, and local attractions.

Bonus Tips:

- Download maps and offline functionality for apps before heading out, as phone reception can be unreliable in remote areas.
- Invest in a waterproof map case or a smartphone waterproof case to protect your navigation resources from the elements.
- Get familiar with basic German phrases, as they can be helpful when interacting with locals or seeking information.
- Check for seasonal closures or restrictions on certain trails before you go.

Remember: These resources are just a starting point. Feel free to explore and discover additional tools and information that suit your specific needs and interests. With the right preparation and resources, your Swiss hiking adventure is sure to be an unforgettable experience!

Happy trails and happy exploring!

Emergency Contact Numbers and Mountain Shelters

Emergency Contact Numbers:

- **General Emergency:** 112 (connects you to the nearest emergency service)
- **Rega (Swiss Alpine Rescue):** 1414 (for emergencies in the mountains)
- **Police:** 117
- **Fire Department:** 118
- **Ambulance:** 144

Mountain Shelters:

Here are some resources to find mountain shelters in Switzerland:

- **SchweizMobil:** Browse through a network of mountain huts with detailed information and locations: https://schweizmobil.ch/en/place-337
- **SAC Schweiz:** Search for mountain huts operated by the Swiss Alpine Club: https://www.sac-cas.ch/en/huts-and-tours/
- **MySwitzerland:** Find information about mountain huts in specific regions: https://www.myswitzerland.com/en/accommodations/other-types-of-accommodations/mountains-huts/
- **Hüttenverzeichnis Schweiz:** Explore a comprehensive directory of mountain huts in Switzerland: https://www.schweizer-huetten.ch/verzeichnis

Additional Tips:

- **Plan your route:** Before you go, choose a trail and identify potential shelters you can reach in case of emergency.
- **Tell someone your plans:** Inform a friend or family member about your route and expected return time.
- **Check opening times:** Mountain huts may have seasonal opening times, so confirm their availability before you go.
- **Be prepared to pay:** Shelters usually charge for meals and overnight stays. Carry enough cash or a credit card.
- **Respect the rules:** Follow the rules and regulations of each mountain hut to ensure everyone's safety and comfort.

Remember: Mountain weather can change quickly, so always be prepared for unexpected situations. Knowing the emergency contact numbers and having access to information about mountain shelters can make a big difference if you encounter any difficulties during your hike.

Stay safe and enjoy your Swiss hiking adventure!

Fold-Out Map of Popular Hiking Regions

Fold-Out Map:

1. **Choose your region:** Which regions in Switzerland are you most interested in exploring? Popular choices include the Bernese Oberland, the Jungfrau Region, the Valais Alps, and Graubünden.
2. **Select your scale:** Do you want a detailed map of a specific area or a more general overview of multiple regions?
3. **Pick your format:** Do you prefer a paper map or a digital version? There are many online map resources available, such as SchweizMobil and MySwitzerland.
4. **Mark your points of interest:** Once you have your map, identify the hiking trails, mountain huts, and other landmarks you want to visit. You can use colored markers, stickers, or annotations depending on the format.
5. **Print or download:** If you choose a paper map, print it out on a large sheet of paper or take it to a printing shop to have it folded and laminated. If you choose a digital version, download it to your phone or tablet.

Recommended Reading List:

Here are some books for deeper alpine exploration, categorized by theme:

Cultural and Historical Exploration:

- "Alpine Wonderland: A History of Mountaineering in Switzerland" by John Harlin
- "Switzerland: A History" by Dick Harrison
- "Swiss Village Life: A Cultural History" by Susan Brownmiller

Nature and Wildlife:

- "Wildlife of the Alps" by David Halliday
- "Flora of the Alps" by Marjory Lack
- "The Alps: A Geological Journey" by Jean-Pierre Piguet

Specific Regions:

- "The Bernese Oberland: A Walking Guide" by Cicerone
- "The Valais Alps: A Hiking Guide" by Sunflower Books
- "Graubünden: A Hiking Guide" by Rother

Bonus Tip: Consider checking out online forums and communities dedicated to hiking in Switzerland. You can connect with other hikers, ask questions, and get recommendations for specific trails and regions.

I hope this helps you create a personalized map and find some inspiring reading material for your Swiss hiking adventure!

Made in the USA
Las Vegas, NV
14 May 2024

89940912R00059